What My "Yes" Cost Me

CORLISS W. COLLINS

Copyright © 2021 by Corliss W. Collins

All rights reserved. No part of this book may be used or reproduced by any means, graphic, electronic, or mechanical, including photocopying, recording, taping, or by any information storage retrieval system, without the written permission of the publisher except in the case of brief quotations embodied in critical articles and reviews.

Editing and Typesetting Services by: TamikaINK.com

Book Cover Design by: KH Designz & Printing LLC

Library of Congress Cataloging – in- Publication Data has been applied for.

Paperback ISBN: 9798487367433

PRINTED IN THE UNITED STATES OF AMERICA.

FIRST EDITION

ACKNOWLEDGEMENTS

First, I would like to thank the lord for keeping me and helping me and loving me and strengthening me through it all. secondly, I would like to give thanks to the love of my life, my husband, Antago. You are my rock, my friend, my heart. I love you. To my beautiful heavenly angel (mom), Vivian Moore. mom, you was with me while I was writing this book. before the book release you was cheering me on. I believe you are looking down on me still cheering me on. mom, I love you more than you would ever know. You will always be my (MVM), most valuable mom. my dad (Ray Webb), you are an awesome dad that any daughter could ask for. I would not trade you for nothing in the world. (I love you dad)! To my awesome sister, Candace Webb you are the best sister ever (I love you sister). To my aunties, uncles, family, friends, and my spiritual leaders that helped me through my ups and downs. I love you family & friends and leaders.

Dear Mom,

    Mom I started writing this book before you took your wings in heaven. I got to admit, Mom, so many nights I would cry out for you to hear your voice and to hug you - just to hear you say, "Keep going you can do this." But with God strengthening me, I, did it, but not in my own strength.
    When you took your wings mom itwas like someone had knock the breathe out of my lungs. But it took God's "Ruach" to revive me to complete the mission.

I love you, Mom.

Dedicated to:
Vivian A. Moore

CONTENTS

Introduction 1

Chapter 1 "What Have I Gotten Myself Into?" 4

Chapter 2 "Meeting Jolly Rancher Man" 9

Chapter 3 "Be Anxious For Nothing" 14

Chapter 4 "The Married Woman With Southern Accent" 20

Chapter 5 "Stop Hitting The Snooze Button" 25

Chapter 6 "Startled Knock At The Door" 31

Chapter 7 "Who Am I?" 35

Chapter 8 "Graduation" 41

Chapter 9 "Pain" 45

Chapter 10 "Death Knocks God Answers The Door." 51

Chapter 11 "Taking Boards" 60

Chapter 12 ("Feeling Empty, Hurt") 63

Chapter 13 ("The Invisible Scars") 72

Chapter 14 ("Override The Knowing") 79

Chapter 15 ("Evidence Vs. Him") 86

Chapter 16 ("He Was The Drug, And I Was The Addict") 95

Chapter 17 ("When The Plan Goes Wrong") 102

Chapter 18 ("Ann's Story") 112

Chapter 19 ("Shattered Dreams") 118

Chapter 20 ("Holding On To Dysfunction") 124

Chapter 21 "Acceptance Phase" 131

Chapter 22 "Rejection Phase" 138

Chapter 23 "Mind Blown Announcement." 144

Chapter 24 (Wrong Response) 151

Chapter 25 ("Wearing Shame Like Makeup") 158

Chapter 26 ("Blue Heart") 163

Chapter 27 ("What's Drawing Me Back") 171

Chapter 28 (My Yes Cost Me) 178

Chapter 29 ("Aborted The Promises") 184

Chapter 30 ("Carrying Out The Mission") 193

Chapter 31 ("Help Me Please, Lord") 200

Chapter 32 ("Catching A Ride With An Angel") 207

Chapter 33 ("Broken Heart's") 213

Chapter 34 ("Strongholds") 220

Chapter 35 (Cost Of Going Back To What God Said "Let Go") 228

Chapter 36 ("Having Victory In A Fixed Fight") 234

Chapter 37 ("Love, Celebrate, Wait") 240

Chapter 38 ("God's Love, And Grace, Forgiveness".) 245

Introduction

"What My Yes Cost Me," is about saying "yes" to the wrong marriage, relationship, the list goes on. Maybe you said "yes" to something that went against everything you once believed in your religion, etc. This "yes" might have cost you heartache, mental breakdown, divorce, lost, or you might be stuck in the middle of your "yes" right now. A true "yes" to the lord and to his will for your life will cause you to break physical and invisible barriers and set you free from your past mistakes such as being entangled in the wrong relationships that you said "yes" to.

This book is about overcoming major obstacles, or circumstances in life. You may appear well put together on the outside, but on the inside, you are tired, torn up, and mentally drained. Your "yes" has you in bondage, and you may feel like it is no coming back from wrong decisions. Maybe you feel like life is just a sour lemon. You feel overlooked, rejected, lonely, and all hope is gone. You may be going through some things that seem uncertain.

I am writing this book to let you know "what my yes cost me!" The Lord set me free from bondage, guilt, shame. The Lord restored my life with his love and grace and mercy, and he is not done yet. When you overcome/come out of "the wrong yes," there is a beautiful, bright, peacefully sunny life. I have to be honest with you, there is a true "yes" in god that is mind blowing. It may cost you. Maybe some friends, sometime away from your favorite T.V. shows, late nights, maybe early morning being with the lord. Whatever cost is in giving God a "yes" to his will for life will be worthy. I'd rather agree to His "yes" than my own yes. The wrong yes in the beginning might have been bad but, the word Ecclesiastes 7:8 "the end of a thing is better than it's beginning," and the best part about that you are not alone in it. Deuteronomy 31:6

"that the lord will never leave you nor forsake you". According to john 10:10(kjv) The thief cometh not, but for to steal, and to kill and destroy: I am come that they might have life, and that they might have it more abundantly." What did your "yes" cost you?

CHAPTER 1

What Have I Gotten Myself Into?

"MA'AM STOP!" I stopped walking and turned around.

"Are you okay ma'am?" He asked.

"Yes, I am," I said.

"I got a call from Andrew. He wanted me to check on you, and plus, there are calls coming in about you," he said.

"Sir, I am okay. This is embarrassing," I said.

"What is embarrassing?" he asked.

"You sir, a Sheriff, stopping me on the side of the highway", I said.

"Did he hit you or anything?" he asked.

"No, he did not," I said.

"Where are you headed? Can I call somebody to come and pick you up?" He asked.

"I am headed to Monroe," I replied.

"That is a long way from here, ma'am", he said.

"I'll be fine", I said.

"Okay are you sure?" he asked again.

"Yes, I am fine thanks!"

"Okay ma'am", he said. He drove off, and I continued walking down the highway.

What we think is our end is really a new beginning only if we let go. In the early 80's, I was born. I grew up in a single parent home with my sister and me in small, country towns. My dad was present in our life. Mom taught us how to be strong, independent women. My mom was my first role model. She inspired us in many ways. She was a beautiful, intelligent, independent, loving, strong woman. My sister and I had no choice but to finish school living under Mom's roof. Mom was not having it at all. Mom took education very seriously; she knew what it took to be successful. After finishing high school, I was inspired by my late aunt who was an RN nurse in St. Louis, Missouri to be a nurse. Along with seeing my mom as a little girl, going back and forth to the hospital. I felt helpless because I could not do anything to help my mom. Seeing that broke me yet inspired me to become a nurse.

At a young age, I thought I was ready to be grown. (Laughing). I felt mom had done enough teaching. Oh, was I wrong? I got married to my high school boyfriend. The marriage later ended in a divorce. Many factors played a role in the divorce. That was a low hit for me. I did not let that stop me. I went on and pursued nursing. While in pursuit of nursing, I also worked as Corporal Officer at the Department of Correction. Even though I was told I was not going to be able to do both nursing school and work by the school counselor. What the counselor did not know, I was not born with a silver spoon in my mouth. I could not afford to stop working and commit totally to nursing. Even though I agreed with the counselor that nursing requires all of one's attention. I could not stop working. In the midst of trying to work and go to nursing school, I was trying not to allow loneliness to take me over. I got tired of men telling me, you are cute but why are you single? As if something was wrong with me. Then, I began to believe the enemy's lies. I allowed him to infiltrate thoughts in my mind. "What is wrong with me? Why am I single? Maybe something is wrong. My ex-husband went on and got remarried." I thought just "maybe" something is wrong.

I came to the conclusion that nothing was wrong with me. Do not believe the lies the devil tells you. Be able to distinguish what voice you are listening too. Allow the Holy Spirit to do the correcting. Ask the Holy Spirit to search every part of your heart. The Holy Spirit will tell you what need to be changed about yourself. See, I thought it was my outer appearance that needed to be changed. Well, it's some truth to that as far as health. Nothing is wrong with fixing your outer appearance but make sure your outer appearance does NOT out-shine your inner appearance. Do not be like a vehicle beautiful on the outside, but the inside engine is messed up. I was a young lady thinking I was ready to jump back into another relationship because I had started fixing my outer appearance.

CHAPTER 2

Meeting Jolly Rancher Man

I woke up every morning, very enthusiastic about being in Nursing School and working. I had been working for the Department of Correction over five years. It came a time when the department was switching out different officers to go work at this prison unit in Tallahassee. I dreaded going to work at Tallahassee unit. My time came when I had to go work 2 weeks at Tallahassee unit. Before going to work, there was a little country store I would stop at to buy candy and chips while working a 12-hr shift. One day on my normal stop at the store, the same lady that would always be behind the counter was there. I spoke to her and walked around to pick up some jolly ranchers and chips. As I walked up to the counter, there was 6'2" tall guy standing at the counter talking with her. He did not appear to be paying for anything, they were just talking. So, I put all my items on the counter. "Can I have some of those jolly ranchers?" he asked. I replied in a sassy way, "No I need all of my candy for tonight." I knew he was doing a little flirting. "I'll pay for it," he went on to say. "No, you don't have too," I said. "Anything you want I'll get it for you," he continued. I thought he was joking when he said that. Before I could give the money to the lady, he handed her the money. "You did not have to pay for it, I had it but thanks," I replied. I picked up my items and headed to the door. He opened the door for me and followed me out to the work vehicle.

"What is your name?" He asked.

"Caroline," I answered, "What is your name?" I asked.

"Andrew," he said, "I knew you had the money to pay for it. You got a man?"

"No, I don't!"

"Can I get your number?" He asked.

We quickly exchanged numbers. I had to get to work. While driving to the unit, I thought why not give him a chance. I am a divorcee and single. Why not jump back into the dating game. *I allowed my emotions to rule over my "waiting period." Don't allow your emotions to rule you. Seek God for a strong discerning spirit before getting involved in any relationship.*

One day while studying in the bathroom. Yes, the thing about nursing, you will find any place to study. My phone rang, and it was a number that I did not recognize. Of course, you know a number you do not know, you let it go to voicemail. I checked my voicemail, "This is Jolly Rancher Man the one you met at the store." In his deep voice, I knew who it was. I did not think anything of it when we exchanged numbers at the store, I didn't lock his number in my phone. I called him back but got no answer. I could not leave a voicemail, because it was full. I just continued studying. Eventually, he and I started talking. Every day that I worked at the Tallahassee Unit, he would meet me at the store. He would pay for my snacks before I went to work. I thought that was very generous of him to do that for me. After talking on the phone with Andrew and being around him, he began to lavish me with whatever I asked him for like he said he would. We both had dreams and goals that we were striving to accomplish. Our relationship began to get stronger and stronger as the days/months went by.

Alone with getting over a divorce. My experience with divorce felt like death to me. It felt like a failure and embarrassment. It left a small stain of pain and hurt in my eyes and heart that only those that were close to me, especially my mom, could see. My smile was my makeup for hurt at the time. Many of us cover our hurt and pain up with some sort of cover up mechanism such as "jokes" or some might say "I'm good" but on the inside just torn apart. Be free release the hurt, pain. The great thing about God he can see right through it and can interpret all of the cover up. He can see things people cannot see. Nothing like being free and authentic when you "smile" and say, "I am good" and really mean it. Waking up to an empty bed took me some time getting use too. I definitely, got tired of holding a pillow every night by myself. I longed to be loved. What I did know is that the void I was feeling, was only to be filled by the Heavenly Father. Sometimes we go through life thinking relationship, money, cars, home, will fill the void. When all we need is his love.

CHAPTER 3

Be Anxious For Nothing

As the relationship between Andrew and I was growing intensely, nursing school was getting hard and harder. I began to question my ability to finish nursing school. Some days it had me wondering maybe the counselor was right about me not being able to do both at the same time. I felt something had to give. Between work or nursing school. I noticed later it drew me to my knees in prayer, along with many other things. I knew I could not do both in my own strength. I put God's word to the test. Philippians 4:13, "I can do all things through Christ that strength me." Or shall I say the word put me to the test. I did not have a clue how God was going to work it out. My mom raised us up in the church, so I knew how to pray.

Sometimes when you pray, it seems as if God is so far away at times. Do not give up, draw in closer to him, and He will draw in closer to you. I learned and still learning that God never intended for us to carry heavy burdens. In 1 Peter 5:7, it tells us "Only to cast our cares upon Him because He cares for you." I thought I did until I found myself worrying about things again.

One day Andrew called me and asked me could he come over to see me? I was not ready for him to come to my apartment but, I was anxious to see him. Even though he and I was talking a lot more and becoming closer, I asked him to meet me at my mom's home. I had already told my mom about where and how I met Andrew. That was not a good idea to let Andrew know where my mom stayed. For safety reason. I was not thinking at all. I gave Andrew the time and address to come over and quickly called my mom to tell her I was on my way over.

Two hours later, I made it to my mom's house. When I stepped out the car, I could smell that fried chicken and spaghetti she was cooking breezing through the screen door by the kitchen. My mom's cooking was the best to me. Along with that grape Kool-Aid and sweet tea she enjoyed making. I loved it! I let her know Andrew was going to stop by to see me, and she did not have a problem with it. Andrew eventually arrived and met my mom as well as my aunt who lived down the street from my mother. We stood outside and talked for a while. We talked about his children and "Papa". I began to tell him what I wanted out of a relationship and vice versa.

"You want to go out to eat?" he asked. I could not believe he would ask me that question. Not because I did not want to go, but he had a friend with him that stayed in the truck while he visited.

"Umm no, I am good, thanks!" I responded. "You have your friend with you in the truck,"

"No, I am going to drop him off," he stated.

"It's okay, my mom cooked already," I replied.

We ended up setting another day and time to go out to dinner. This time he was by himself, just him and me. He met me at mother's house again. He took me out to this restaurant, "Benihana." After we finished dinner, we left the restaurant. He opened the door for me being a gentleman. While heading down the street to get on the highway, we started talking.

He asked me, "Am I going home with you?"

"Yeah, you can," I replied. He drove a totally opposite way to his house. When we pulled up at his house, he jumped out the truck.

"I'll be right back," he said.

"Okay", I stated.

I saw a couple of guys hanging around the house smoking cigarettes, I assumed. Andrew returned from the house with a little night bag in his hand. We drove back to my mom's house to pick up my car. He followed me over to my apartment. As we entered my apartment, I told him he could have a seat on the couch and handed him the remote to the T.V. That night I knew nothing was going to happen, he laid on one side of the bed, and I laid on the other side. Around 3a.m., Andrew's phone went off. He jumped up as if someone had thrown cold water on him, rushing to put on his clothes. He was in a hurry as if he was late for something.

"Is everything okay?" I asked.

"Yeah, I got to get back to Tallahassee," he responded. I thought that was a little strange for him to be rushing back, but I walked him to the door. "I'll call you later today," he said.

I closed the door behind him, locked it and got back in the bed. Later on, that day, Andrew called me. "When can you come and spend the night with me in Tallahassee?" he questioned.

"Umm, between studying and working, I don't know", I said.

"You can bring your homework with you."

"Okay."

"I can come pick you up."

"Alright! On my short week of working, yeah that's fine", I said.

"Alright."

I am not going to lie I was anxious about spending more time with him. *Don't be anxious about anything!!! The only thing you should be anxious about is God promises and the great things he has in store for you. Philippians 4:6-8 "Do not be anxious about anything", but in every situation, prayer and petition". I did not pray at all. I just jump right into this relationship.*

CHAPTER 4

The Married Woman with Southern Accent

The following week came for me to spend the night at Andrew's house. I was still anxious about spending the night. I called mom and told her that I was going to spend the night in Tallahassee with Andrew.

"Carolina, be careful, call me when you make it down there," she said. "Take it slow, Carolina. You just got out of a divorce, now you are jumping into something else." I knew my mom concern was coming from a good place. "Okay," I said. Later that night, Andrew came by the apartment to pick me up. We headed down to Tallahassee. We were laughing and joking all the way.

Once we made it to his house, he took my bag and opened the car door for me. As I walked inside his house, I saw a big, beautiful picture of him and a little girl. "Is that your daughter?" I asked. "Yeah, that is my baby," he replied. "You can have a sit. Ain't nothing going to bite you," he said laughing. "Where is your restroom?" I asked. I tried to call my mom while I was in the restroom, but my phone was not picking up a signal. I began to scream on the inside. How can I call anyone if my phone is not picking up a signal? I washed my hands and came out the bathroom. I walked back and sat on the couch.

"You want something to eat?" he asked. "Yeah," I said. He started cooking. We ate and started talking. "I need to study, I have an exam coming up," I said. "Go ahead don't let me bother you," he replied. As we were sitting in the house, I saw vehicle head lights come through the living room window. Next, I heard a car door slam. He looked over at me, and I look back at him. I picked up my phone to check the time; it was 10p.m. I was thinking it is a little late for some company. He rushed to the front door and walked out to the porch. I closed my textbook. I heard a female voice but was not sure who was visiting him this time of night. He told me that he was single, so I knew it was not a girlfriend. Minutes later, a female comes walking in the front door. She looked at me, and I looked at her. She spoke in this deep southern voice63, and I spoke back. By this time, I noticed she still was standing in the middle of the living room. I am thinking okay are we going to have to fight. I looked over at him, like who is this. She looks at him and ask him a question.

"Who is this, Andrew?" she asked. As if I'm not still present in the living room. Rude.

"Ask her who she is," he said.

"Who are you? Are you, his girlfriend?" she asked in her deep southern accent.

"I am his friend," I said.

"Man, get out of here woman," he told her. "Don't come down here starting no mess," he said. "Man, you are a married woman. Why do you care who I am seeing?"

They both started walking outside. At this point, I'm feeling really silly. I did not drive my own car. Five minutes later, he walked back in and apologized. "I apologize for that, "he said.

"Look, I don't like being in no mess. You told me that you were single," I said.

"I am single, she is just somebody I stopped seeing," he said.

"I don't like being a part of any drama and look like you got that going on. Do you mind taking me home?" I asked.

"Yeah, I don't mind taking you home, but can I take you home in the morning?" he asked.

"Yeah", I said.

I wish would have driven my own car. We went to bed, but I did not sleep well at all. That just did not sit well with me. The next morning, I grabbed my night bag and headed to the bathroom to freshen up. He was standing in the kitchen cooking breakfast.

"Good morning, Carolina!" he said.

"Good morning, Andrew!" I said. I continued walking to the bathroom. I was ready to go home. When I came out of the bathroom, he had breakfast ready for us to eat. While eating breakfast, he stated, "I apologize for what happen last night, it's really nothing with that woman. She is a married woman. I did not even know she was going to come over here."

"Okay", I said. I was ready to leave at this point. I took him at his word. I overrode what I felt on the inside to satisfy my fleshly desires.

CHAPTER 5

Stop Hitting the Snooze Button

I felt something was not right the night before. We continue talking all the way to my apartment. Andrew kept pleading his case that the lady was full of it. We made it back to my apartment. I grabbed my backpack from the backseat.

"Can I call you later today?" He asked.

"Yeah", I said. I close the car door and walk to my apartment.

The last thing I needed in my life was drama. I had enough going on in my personal life. But he could be telling the truth. I briefly stopped calling and texting Andrew because I was battling with believe him or not. We needed to get some air between us. Plus, I needed to stay focus on nursing. A week later, I reached out to

Andrew to see what he had going on. I missed talking with him. He and I ended up linking up. This time, it involved a little more than talking. After months had passed without any drama. I ended up going back to Tallahassee spending the night with him.

We decided we were going to make the relationship official. We picked up like nothing had ever happen. He started coming over to my apartment spending the night. One evening, riding home from class Andrew called me. I had excitement every time he called me.

"Hey, what are you doing?" He asked.

"Just leaving class," I said.

"Are you coming to Tallahassee tonight?" He asked.

"Yes!" I was like that high school girl all over again.

I had fallen in love all over again, I was excited about my new man. The relationship was good. Fresh new love! I began to leave toothbrush and little things at his house. Claiming territory to show he has a woman. Which is the silliest thing to do as I look back at it. We had hiccups in the relationship every now and then, nothing serious.

The stronger our relationship grew, the stronger the sex grew. I began to feel like he belongs to me and only me, no one else. There is a reason why God tells us not to have sex before marriage. You become so emotionally involved with the wrong person, creating ungodly soul ties. God knows the end and the beginning of everything. Never let your flesh and emotions trick you into doing what is wrong because you will pay for it later.

My Pastor taught us Holiness. So, when I started having sex with Andrew, Sunday would come, and I would sit in the far back of the church. Thinking, maybe the back bench could hide my sin; not so. The thing about a true man/woman prophet/prophetess, you cannot pull anything over them. They can see the sin. Prophet comes to edify, exhort, and comfort (1 Corinthians). And the best part they work for the Lord, not people. And you cannot buy them. NEVER underestimate the Power that works within them.

I got so entangled with Andrew, the relationship began to pull me away from God which was/is dangerous thing to do. Exodus 20:3-5 "thou shalt have no other gods before me." Andrew had become, my god. I would leave in the middle of church service, sometimes, if he called and told me he was on his way over to my place. A year had passed and here I was still tackling nursing school and a new relationship. When I was not working or going to class, I was in Tallahassee with Andrew.

One my day off, I decided to call Andrew to see what he had going on for the night. I got no answer. A lot of the time when Andrew would not answer the phone, at some point during the day, he would eventually call me back. But this day he did neither a text nor phone call. I waited patiently all day. The alarm went off on the inside of me, I shook it off. It's nothing.

It's just me overthinking. I ignored the unction like an alarm clock you hit when you are not ready to wake up.

As the days went by, Andrew decided to tell me why he was unable to answer the phone. He was painting a house, and he never got around to calling me back. I believed him. I did not doubt him, but it became the new normal for our relationship because he began to pick up more work. One day, I decide to do a "pop up" along with me spending the night down at his house. We know what a "pop up" is: coming over without calling. Or you called that person, and they did pick up the phone. And you decide to show up. I had called him, but he did not pick the phone. The old saying is, "Don't do that if you do not want your feelings hurt." I was willing to take the chance because he would always reassure me nothing was going on. That ole saying did not apply to me that day. Our relationship was good. I figured I was just in competition with his working hours. But, deep on the inside I kept pushing down what I felt. Sometimes we don't think it's the Holy Spirit trying to tell us something is off. We don't know it's God at the time. We might say "Something told me". Never override the Holy Spirit.

Stop hitting the snooze button on your relationship, the alarm (Holy Spirit) is going off for a reason for you to wake up.

CHAPTER 6

Startled Knock at the Door

I jumped in my car, headed to the gas station to put gas in my car. I was heading down to Tallahassee to have a talk with Andrew and to spend some time with him. I started feeling some fluttering in my stomach. While on my way to his house, Andrew decided to call me back before I could "pop up."

"Hello," I said.

"I saw you called what's up?" He asked.

"I'm on my way down there," I replied.

"Okay," he said, calmly.

We hung up the phone. I made it to his house. I got my things out of the car. I walked in the house. "Hey babe", he said. I felt so silly thinking I was going to find something. I went to the bathroom to make sure my toothbrush was still where I put it alone with some other items. Everything was there. I was relieved to find out everything that I was feeling, and thinking was wrong. We started talking about our day. He was telling me how he had picked up some extra work. Time went on, and it was getting late. I went to the bathroom and took a shower. Shortly after, he went to the bathroom to take a shower. Andrew and I was laying in the bed moments later, after he and I just finished having sexual intercourse. We heard a knock on the front living room window. We both were startled by the hard knock at the window. I'm thinking who knocks on a living room window. He got up and walked into the living room. I walk with him to front door. He pulled the door behind him. I look through the front window to see who was there. The car was parked on the side of the street. I heard a lady screaming at the top of her lungs, "Andrewwww, who is in the house?" While she was yelling, she was trying to get inside of the house. She was fighting him trying to gain entrance in the house. He picked her up and forced her back into the car. I saw when he opened the car door as the car dome light came on inside the car. There was a dark-skinned lady who was not the same lady that came by the first night I was over here. I'm saying to myself, this cannot be happening again!

Andrew came stomping back in the house. Breathing hard, he had shame and guilt all over him. His face had turned red. I looked at him and walk to the bedroom and started putting my clothes on. He sat on the side of the bed.

"It's nothing like that man." He started to repeat.

"Andrew, who is that?" I asked. A question that her and I both wanted to know.

"She's just a woman that stays down the street that likes me. Man, that lady is on drugs," he said.

"On drugs, Andrew, really?" I said.

"Don't leave it's too late for you to be on the highway. Baby, it's late, and it's dark on the highway," he said.

I yelled, "No, Andrew that is not just some woman down no street! On drugs! That lady had too much rage to be just some lady."

I left that night heading down the dark highway back to my apartment. I was hurt, angry, and all of these emotions were all over the place. My phone rung, and it was Andrew. I hit 'ignore' on the phone. After not picking up the phone, he sent a text message, "Caroline come back." I took the phone and threw it down on the passenger floor. After driving back in anger, I made it safe to my apartment, crawled in the bed, and put the sheets over my head and cried myself to sleep.

CHAPTER 7

Who Am I?

RING, RING! I look at my phone, it was my mom.

"Hey, little girl," she said.

"Hey mom!"

"Do you have to go to work tonight?" She asked.

"Yeah, mom. Can I call you when I get up, mom?"

"Bye, little girl", she said. We said our love you and we got off the phone.

I went through my phone, and I had missed calls and texted messages from Andrew. I was not trying to hear anything he had to say at all. But I wanted to get some answers out of him. This week was my long week to work, and I tried to stay focus on nursing school and not fail any of my classes. The following week came. I went down to Tallahassee to speak with Andrew about what happen. I pulled up to the house and noticed a couple of vehicles in the yard. I knocked on the door, and a guy opens the door for me. I walked into the house and see some guy hanging around in the kitchen with him talking. "Hey, can I talk with you outside, Andrew?" I asked. "Yeah," he replied. We walked outside.

"Andrew, what is really going on with our relationship?" I asked.

"Nothing. It is you tripping, babe. Only if you knew," he said.

"What does that mean Andrew?"

"I'm not with anybody but you, Carolina. I told you that lady is crazy," he said. I was shaking my head in no position. "What does that mean, Carolina?" He asked.

"I've got to get back home and study. I've got exams coming up," I said. He put his arms around me, hugged me, and kiss me on the forehead. I left heading back home, leaving like I came, "empty."

Heading back home to study, I had to switch my focus back on nursing school. While studying hard and praying. I felt this guilt that would come over me at times about praying, because I was not living the Christ life like I should've. I didn't fully understand God's grace and mercy at the time. Not to sin. But to be set free from sin. I was so grateful to find out that I had passed the first part of Nursing. With the many exams one after another, I would be a nervous wreck before taking the exams and afterwards. Along with dealing with Andrew and our relationship, I did not think I would have any nerves left to finish Nursing. I was praying that I pass all the exams. It got to the point where I had to move back in with my mom. The stress in nursing school began to be too much for me. I still had bills, and small fees that came with nursing school. I still had to work.

My mom allowed me to move back in with her which I was truly so grateful. My mom was my #1 cheerleader, cheering me on. She knew how important it was for me to finish nursing school. Andrew and I was still seeing each other despite the past drama he had going on. He helped me move some of my furniture into a smaller storage and some at a building that he was currently using for storage himself. It got to the point where I started to accept any, and everything he would do. I would talk with my mom and my sister about what was going on with me in school. I knew I could call my BFF on the phone and tell her what was going on in my relationship. Like any BFF would, she had a zero tolerance for him. My mom, sister shared some of the same feelings about Andrew. My mom would tell me just leave him alone. I think it hurt my family and many others as to who the person I had turned into. How could somebody be this smart, and strong and allow such nonsense to go on and not let go. Needless to say, I did not have an answer to those questions.

In May 2009, I was standing in my mom's bathroom looking in the mirror at someone that is bright in one area, yet weak and naïve in another. I had finished getting ready for work and class. It was my last exam to take for nursing. Afterwards, I had head to work. I was mentally trying to prepare myself to stay focused on the exam, not Andrew or work. Nothing had changed in Andrew and our relationship. He was still up to the same, old games. It was crunch time for me, I had to give it my all on this last exam. On my way out the house my mom yelled, "Good luck, you can do it!" I replied, "Thanks, mom! Love you, pray for me. I'll see you in the morning."

Locking the door behind me. I made it into the classroom, and I said a prayer before taking the exam. I scanned the room looking around at some of my nursing colleagues' faces. It was the intenseness we all had on our face that told a story within itself. After I finished taking my exam, I walked out into the hallway and drank some water from the fountain. We were watching the instructor walk out the classroom to grade the exams. We knew when the instructor would walk back into the class, it was time to go back into the class.

I am not sure about my classmates, but I tried to look at instructor's facial expression to determine if we, as a class, did well. This time I could not tell. "When I call your name, you can come and get your exam," she said. Once we had gotten our exam, we could leave quietly after class. When she called my name to come and get my exam, my knees were shaking all the way there and back to my seat. I looked down at my paper. I PASSED my exam! On my way out of the door, I called my mom.

"Mom, I passed the exam!" I exclaimed.

"Hayyy, you go girl," she said.

"Okay, mom, I'm headed to work."

"Okay, love you," she said.

I called Andrew to tell him about the good news before going into work. I got no answer!

CHAPTER 8

Graduation

I made it home from work, still excited about passing the nursing school exam. Now, it was time for me to prepare for graduation. I did not tell my dad about my graduation because I was not sure if I was going to pass my last exams or not. I did not want him traveling from Texas for nothing. I told him. My dad was happy for me. After a long night of working a long 12 hours, I needed to get some rest. I set my alarm clock to go off at 2p.m. so I would not sleep all day. Before I went to sleep my sister, Jenny, called me.

"Hey, Carolina, mom told me you passed. Congratulations!!"

"Thanks, Jenny," I said.

"I know you just got off work, call me when you wake up." We hung up the phone.

Still no call back from Andrew. I was too sleepy to worry about it. My alarm clock went off, I was not ready to get up, so I just laid in bed for a second. I picked up my phone and saw Andrew had texted me. I texted back and asked him to call me. He did not call me right away, but he did call.

"Hello Carolina, what's up with you?" He asked.

"Well, I called you last night to let you know I had passed nursing," I said.

"Oh, congratulations, babe!"

"Thanks, Andrew."

"What are you fixing to get into?"

"Nothing."

"Let me call you back okay, babe?"

"Okay," I said.

We hung up the phone.

After hanging up the phone with Andrew, I was in awe about how God worked everything out that I was worrying about. He allowed me to work as a correctional officer while studying nursing at the same time. Nobody but God could have done that. He had the right people at the right place, at the right time. His word says in Matthew 19:26, *"With man this is impossible, but with God, all things are possible"*. I am a living witness of his word. I know it was God that brought me through it all. Whatever looks impossible to you, seek God and His guidance. Because when he says, "Yes" and puts His hands on it, watch him move on your behalf. Have faith in God. Sometimes we, as people, have a hard time "Resting in God" (Hebrew 4:9) and entering in God's rest. To enter in God's rest is the best thing any human can do.

While I was still engulfed in the excitement of making it through nursing school, so were my mom, dad, family/friends, and co-workers also. Graduation night I was happy to see the support of my family/friends, co-workers, and Andrew for showing up. The mini party gathering we had at mom's house ended short for me because I left my own party to go and stay the night with Andrew. One of my co-workers that always crack jokes with me said, "Umm yeah, we should have known once Andrew showed up, you were going to leave. BYE!" We both laughed. Before I left, I gave hugs and kisses and thanked all who came out to celebrate my accomplishment.

CHAPTER 9

Pain

I was so busy running behind Andrew, giving into my flesh. Romans 7:18 "For I know that in me (that is, in the flesh,) dwelleth no good thing." The thing about sin, it makes you feel so shameful, guilty and ugly. I had gotten myself so intertwined and committed to the wrong yes, I lost myself in the midst.

1 Corinthians 6:18, *"Flee from sexual immorality. All other sins a person commits are outside the body, but whoever sins sexually, sins against their own body."* I was sinning against my own body. I was inflicting pain upon my body. Instead of sitting and studying for Nursing Boards, I was too busy ripping up and down the highway chasing after Andrew. December 2009 is when my whole life spiraled out of control. Nothing could have prepared me or my family mentally for what was

What My "Yes" Cost Me

coming my way. It was the evening around Christmas time, my mom and I drove to my Aunt Lisa's house. Sometimes my aunt, uncle, and family would get together around the holidays and eat and joke around. We were having the greatest time. It was getting late. I knew if we left and headed back home during this time of night, it would be hard to see deer on the highway. Deer are bad during this time of the year in this state. Mom and I decided to spend the night at my Aunt Lisa's and Uncle Danny's house. I was getting tired after telling jokes and just having fun with family, so I made me a comfortable pallet, and I went to sleep.

I woke up to the most excruciating pain in my stomach. The pain was so intense it literally woke me up out of my sleep. I jumped up placing my hand on my stomach. With grunting sound, I was making from the pain, my mom woke up.

"What's wrong with you?" She asked.

"My stomach, mom, it hurts really bad. We've got to go, mom," I said.

"Are you going to be able to drive?" She asked.

"I don't know. I can try," I said.

"Just wait, I spoke with your cousin last night. She is supposed to be coming this morning."

"Okay," I replied.

I called my cousin, Tammy, to see how far away she was. She told me she would be here in 15 minutes. I asked her if she mind taking me to the hospital. She had no problem taking me to the hospital. The only problem with that was there was a particular hospital that I wanted to go to which was 30 minutes away. Fifteen minutes turned into 5 minutes because I heard Tammy, walking through the door. I got up, and we headed to the hospital.

"What happened?" She asked.

"I don't know if it was something I ate or what, but this is a pain I have never felt before."

My cousin, Tammy, got me to the hospital quickly and safely. She pulled me up to the emergency door. As

I made it to the door, the nurse asked if I needed a chair to sit in. "Yes, please," I responded. She took my information and put a wrist band on my arm and wheeled me over to the side. She told me they would be calling me to the back shortly.

Tammy, walked in later and sat with me. I was frightened because I did not know what was going on with me. They eventually called my name, Tammy followed me to the back. Tammy called my mom, giving her the update. The nurse told me to slip into my gown, and she would be right back to start the IV. They were going to run some test. The doctor, Jack, came in and told me that he was going to give me something for pain and run some test. They gave me something for the pain. We were still sitting and waiting on the results to come back. It seemed like hours had gone by. The doctor returned and grabbed a chair and took a deep breath and slowly exhaled.

"Hi, I'm Dr. Jack, as I mention earlier," he said. "Well, looks like you are going to have to do an emergency surgery." WHAT?! SURGERY! I never had any surgery. The only thing I was used to was needles.

"Can you give a pill or something, instead of surgery? Is that the only option on the table?" I asked.

"No ma'am. The only option right now is surgery. That's going to be the safest thing for you right now."

"Okay", I said. Tammy called my mom and told her, and she headed to the hospital. I didn't want my mom driving at all.

My cousin, Tammy, was a little taken aback by the surgery just as much as I was. She stayed with me the whole time. The nurse came back in and told me that they were getting a room ready for me. I called Andrew to tell him what happen. No answer! I felt this was the worse time for him not to be pick up the phone. I had no time to be upset. My mom made it to the hospital and did not leave. They prepared a room for me. While we were waiting for the doctor to come and speak with me, I told my mom and cousin, Tammy, I was afraid to have surgery. "I know you are," Mom said. That night, the doctor wanted me to make up in my mind quickly when I was ready to have surgery. He said it did not have to be tonight but soon. I was so resistant about having surgery, but they stressed the fact that it was a common surgery and nothing to be afraid of. The next morning, I agree to the surgery.

CHAPTER 10

Death Knocks God Answers The Door

I was trying to wake up. Every time I would open my eyes, I would see my mom with tears running down her face, shaking her head. I could hear sounds. The disbelief she had on her face. I wanted to say something, but I could not. I was not sure if I was dreaming or if this was real. I attempted to wake up again. I tried to move. I heard Mom say, "Carolina don't move baby." I was confused as to why I could not keep my eyes open and trying to figure out if this was a bad dream I was having. I wanted to come out of whatever I was in. Later, I found out while being in surgery, the surgery went wrong. Bad wrong. Death was knocking at my door. They had me heavily medicated. I could hardly catch up to what was going on at one point. I was not sure what day/month it was. With the many attempts of me trying to come to myself, I was finally able to open my eyes. I looked over at my mom. I was looking around the room. "Mom, what happened to me?" I asked. She could hardly tell without crying. "Baby, you are messed up. Just try not to move," she said.

With the many surgeries I had to go through, there would be times when the nurse and doctors wanted me to eat. Food was the last thing on my mind. The pain was drowning out my taste buds for food. When my mom or cousin would come to visit me, I would save my food for them, depending on the time either one would come to visit. Sometimes it would be lunch or dinner. I gave it to them. It did not take long before the nurses and doctors caught on to what was going on. The food trays were empty, but I was still losing weight. I remember my dad coming back and forth to see me and spending the night at the hospital. My mom, dad, sister, BFF, uncles, and aunties came in local and from out of town. They transferred me to another hospital that could handle the type of trauma I had experience.

I remember Andrew came to the hospital to bring me a teddy bear and balloons. I was excited to see him.

"What happened, Babe?" He asked. I only told him the little bit of information I could remember.

"Look like they messed you up, Babe. "Why they got all these tubes coming out of you?" Are you going to get an attorney?" He asked.

"I don't know," I said.

I could not answer the question about an attorney being involved at the time. That was the last thing on my mind. This was a day-to-day thing for me. I didn't want to die. With the many facial expression that were hiding behind their smiles, I could see hurt/sadness on some of my family's faces. My mom could not hold back the hurt she was feeling. Mom was right beside me. My dad was hurt also. The traveling back and forth he did to come and see me. The nights he would spend night at the hospital. My sister, Jenny, was so light skinned that when she came in the room, her little nose and eyes would be red. She could not hide it at all either. The support I had from my uncles and aunts that travel near and far, and the countless times my BFF and her husband drove back and forth to come see me was priceless. I was grateful for the support. If I was going to die at least I was able to see my family and friends before leaving this earth.

I had to go through multiple surgeries. The back and forth of surgeries went on for about 3 years, but the doctors and nurses were not sure if I was going to pull through this last repair that lasted 7 hours in surgery with a blood transfusion. After the major surgery, I went into a deep depression. I was in a dark place. I did not understand it. My mom had to bathe me and turn me at night, change my dressing, you name it, Mom did it. Along with her having to go to work. I would cry when my leave the room. I saw the hurt my mom had on her face. I love my mom. She had strength like no other woman I know. I was crying on the inside and out. It was a cry that only God could interpret. In my mind, I was now confused about God. Why did this happen to me? I would sometimes think if God loved me, then why did he allow this to happen? The great thing about what God allows to happen in our life. He knows what is on the other side of the situation. Have I been considered like JOB in the bible? Surely not, JOB feared God, stayed away from evil, and he walked upright before the Lord. Or was this payback for being in sin with Andrew?

They told me I would have to go for a lifetime of follow up with a specialist doctor. That just added more darkness to what I was already thinking. God had to renew my mind. I'm living now and God made death behave on my behalf. So, I had to make a choice to be thankful and grateful. I, now, had to accept that my inside anatomy is not like a normal person anatomy now. I thought about how God was going to pull me through this and what was afterwards. I could not see what was going to happen. I remember my auntie gave me this little red book with nothing but bible verses. Even though I was speaking the word. I was still feeling like all hope was gone. My dad would say. It's a silver lining at the end of the tunnel. Well, for me it was dark. I did not see color at the end of the tunnel at all. I had not taken my Nursing Boards. I felt all of my hard work of going to nursing school had gone down the drain. I knew it had to be prayers from my mom/dad, pastor, family members, and friends that kept me.

I kept that little red book in the bed with me. I began to speak healing bible verses. At first, it felt like words just on a page until I began to see myself getting my strength back and my healing started. The Word was my medicine. The doctors couldn't do anything else to help. They hope the surgery worked out. Not knowing for sure. We all were praying. It was up to God now. I did not stop taking the pain medicine the physical doctors had prescribed for me. The Lord had now introduced himself to me as JEHOVAH ROPHI (The

Lord My Healer). It was two wars going on with me, maybe even three. One was mental, and the other, physical healing. At times, Andrew would come by and visit me. Sometimes he would encourage me that it was going to get better. Time went by, I started back walking again. My eating started to get back on track. I knew then that the bible was NOT just mere WORDS printed in a book, but the true LIVING Word of God and was real to me. I knew it was not the medicine from the doctors because that medicine kept the pain away and me, sleepy. I did not want to get too excited because it would be times, I still did not want to be left alone because I was still battling with the thoughts of the *how, why, and what ifs,* the enemy was trying to place in my mind. I would think about how I was going to pass the Nursing Boards. Years had passed. There was no way I was going to be able to remember any of the material I was taught in school with all the medicine and trauma, I had gone through and still having tubes hanging outside of my stomach with a bag attached to me. My mind was too foggy to remember anything. Some days

I still could not fathom in my mind how did I get here. The enemy would still, whisper things like if God loves you then why would he allow this to happen? Some days, I would agree with him because I fell back into a deep depression, worrying.

If you are going through dark moments in your life, do not allow the enemy to whisper lies in your ear. Let devil know "IT IS WRITTEN," Matt. 4:11. I was so worried about my life and so was my mom. When you are going through some dark/hopeless moments in your life, it is important to have the Word of God right beside you and in your heart and some true intercessors that can pray for you, pray you through, and keep you covered in prayer. Not just say it, but truly pray for you.

Mom finally found an attorney that took a load off her and me tremendously. Andrew began to call me without me having to call him. This lifted me up. Andrew really took a different approach with our relationship. I started taking steps to take the board exams. Not sure if I was going to pass or not, but I wanted to try. Some days I would be at home and would begin to negotiate with God about bringing me out of what I was going through.

Have you ever found yourself trying to negotiate with God? I would say, "God, if you just do this, I will do that or this." What I did not know was that I did not need to negotiate with him. God cared more about me, and every detail of my life much more than I did. He knows all and sees all, Psalms 139:2-6.

CHAPTER 11

Taking Boards

Things began to get back to normal for me. I started back driving again. I went ahead and registered to take the Nursing Board's exam. I felt like I had done enough studying. The day came for me to take the exam. That morning before I took the boards, I prayed all the way to place and back home. I remembered when the instructors would tell us in class, just because the computer shuts off at 75 or goes all the way to the full 200 questions, it does not mean you have passed the boards. I walked into the building. I got a locker and put all my things in until I finished the test. I walked in the computer room, and I immediately froze at the computer. For a moment, I was just staring at the time clock in the upper corner. I took a deep breath and took my time. I answered the questions to the best of my ability. I made it to question 75 and the computer shut off. Oh, my goodness was I nervous screaming on the inside! I was not sure what I had scored on the exam. Days later I could go online and check to see if I had passed the boards. It was mid-week, I got on the computer praying that I had passed. I could not get the computer to act right to see if I had passed or not. So, I had to call to get some assistance with it. After getting the assistance, finally, I was able to pull up my name. I had passed the boards! "YES!" I was screaming. Oh, my goodness. Thank you, Lord! He did it again!! I know the Lord as YAHWEH now. There was no way I could have passed the boards after 2 years of being out of nursing school and with going through what I had gone through. No way possible. I remember after graduation; the instructors were encouraging the students to go ahead and take the boards so we would not forget what we were taught. It was entirely too much information to try and retain and go back and relearn. But God showed His mighty hand!!! Now, it was time to get a job. I was determined to push pass every obstacle that I had faced along with the tubes I still had. I had started putting applications online and in person. The bills were overdue, and I needed to get something going for myself. My relationship with Andrew was still steady at that point. His truck began to give him problems, so I agreed to let him use my car until he found another vehicle. If we would just look at the Lord and not the problem. He is the Great "I Am who I Am".

CHAPTER 12

Feeling Empty, Hurt

I called Andrew to let him know I was coming there to spend the night with him. He did not answer the phone. I was still super excited that I had passed the boards. I could not wait to see him. Now that I had become a nurse, something that I once inspired to be as a little girl, the excitement was not going away anytime soon. It was excitement all around me even with Andrew and our relationship, it was like we never skipped a beat. I continued to let him drive my car. I could not afford to have my car repossessed. I was in the middle of finding a job and trying to get on my feet. My mom allowed me to drive her car until this court case got settle for my injury. Before heading to see Andrew, I called him a second time to see if he wanted something to eat before

I arrived there. I called and he picked up on the first ring.

"Hello," he said.

"Hey, Andrew!"

"What are you doing?" He asked.

"I am headed there, but I am going to stop and get me something to eat first. Do you want anything?"

"Yeah, where are you going?" He asked.

"I'm going to pick up a burger."

"Okay, yeah pick me up one too."

"Okay," I replied.

After picking up our food, I headed to Tallahassee. While driving to Tallahassee, I was thinking about how well our relationship was going and if I needed to bring up to him about marriage. I knew he had already told me that we were going to get married, but I am not going to lie, I was anxious about when. Have you ever been anxious in a relationship about when the one you love will pop the big question? Or when you will get married? Perhaps, you are single or in a relationship waiting and wondering, when will the day come? I did not want to keep asking him when, when? Every time I would ask him, it seemed as if asking him would agitate him. Or he would come up with something like, "It is coming." Geesh!

I made it to Tallahassee. I pulled up in the yard, but I did not see my car in the yard. I pulled out my phone and called Andrew to let him know I made it to his house. Before I made it completely out of the car, I saw head lights from a vehicle coming down the street. Andrew parked my car on the side of the street.

"Hey!" I turned around and it was Andrew getting out the car, walking up to the front door to let me in. "I had to run down the street before you made it down here."

"What's going on down the street?" I asked.

"I had to go drop something off to my uncle."

"Oh okay," I said. I handed him the food, while I went back to the car to get my night bag. I walked back in the house and took my clothes to the bedroom.

"How are you feeling?" He asked.

"I feel okay this tube hurts sometimes, but I'm fine."

"When are they going to remove it?" He asked.

"I'll know next month," I said. We sat on the couch and started eating our food.

"Have you heard anything back from your attorney yet?" He asked.

"Yeah." I did not go into details about what my attorney had discussed, and he did not ask me anything else after that. We finished eating our food. We both looked at each other with full bellies.

"You're full?" He asked.

"Yep", I'm going to take a shower," I said.

I got up from the couch and went to the bedroom to get my clothes to take a shower. I walked to bathroom and took a shower. After taking a shower, I went back into the living room and sat down, and we continued to talk.

"What's going on with the building, Andrew?" I asked.

"We got to do some more work on it, Babe," he said. It appeared that he really was not interested in talking about the building. He got up from the couch and walked to the bedroom and grabbed him some undergarments and went to the bathroom to take a shower.

Later that night, he and I had sexually relations. Afterwards, I went to the bathroom and took a shower. Something felt different about the night. I sensed it, it was calm feeling that I never felt spending the night over his house. After taking a shower, I got in the bed with him, and we went to sleep. I woke up to Andrew standing in the closet putting on his clothes, with him rushing as usually. Andrew always woke up as if he was late for an appointment.

"I'll be back. Lock the door if I'm not back before you leave," he said.

"Okay," I responded.

I really could not go back to sleep once he left. An hour later, I got out of the bed and went to the bathroom to get dressed. I locked the door behind me and left headed back to mom's house. I pulled into the parking lot and texted Andrew to let him know I made it home safely before getting out the car. Once I made it inside the apartment, I went to my room and grabbed a saline flush and sat on the couch to flush the tube. After flushing the tube, I laid on the couch for a second because the tube started bothering me. It was not unusual for that to happen after flushing the tube.

Later that night, my mom and I went to get something to eat. When we made it back home, I noticed he never did respond to the text I sent him earlier that morning. I texted Andrew to see what he was up to again. I still did not get a response back. Maybe Andrew is working, I will give him time to call me back.

Later that night, I realized Andrew still had not called or texted me back from earlier. I'm sure our relationship is not going backwards. I called him around 10 o'clock p.m. His phone went straight to his voice mail. Not again because we were doing good. I tried not to think the worse. I felt like we had overcome pettiness. Even though I was trying to talk myself out of thinking the worse. I felt like something was going on, but I was not sure what it was. An hour later, I called his phone again. His phone went directly to his voice mail again. I could not leave him a voice mail because his voicemail was always full. At 12 a.m., I went to my mom's room to ask her if I could use the car for a second. She said yes.

I got in the car and headed down to Tallahassee. While I was driving all types of thoughts were going on in my head. Is he with another woman? What am I going see when I get down there? Will I be like that first lady that came over the first night I was at his house? Am I going to be the other woman on the other side of the door now? I mean all these thoughts were flowing through my mind while I was driving. I made it to Tallahassee. When I turned onto the street where the house was, I saw some guys hanging around on the corner. I pulled up to the house, but I did not see my car in the front yard. I got out the car and walked up to door and knocked. I did not see lights or TV on in the house. I walked around to the back of the house and knocked on the back door. Still no answer. Nor did I see my car in the back yard. I walked back to the car and sat inside the car and looked down at my phone. I sent him a text message. "Where are you?" Still no response. I saw Bill coming up the street on his bicycle. Bill was Andrew's go-to guy. He would do little odds and end work around the house for Andrew. I rolled down the driver side window.

"Bill, where is Andrew?" I asked.

"He's not at home," he said.

"I know that." I looked down at my phone. It was 2 a.m. in the morning. "Okay," I said. I let the window back up. I laid my head back on the seat trying to hold back the tears from falling. I felt empty, hurt on the inside.

CHAPTER 13

The Invisible Scars

I left Tallahassee heading home, crying, because I felt that he was with another woman, but I had no proof. Just when I thought our relationship was getting better, it was like the relationship took 10 steps backwards. As I was traveling down this dark highway with this hurt, there were hardly any cars on the highway. The huge moon was lighting up the sky. It was a full moon that night. As the tears were filling in my eyes, I was asking why? Why did I feel so hurt and lonely? Why would he do this to me?

Have you ever been so hurt by person emotionally that you were in denial of what was happening to you? This was me. The hurt had cut me deep. It left an invisible scar of hurt on my heart.

I made it home, turned the key in the door, went into my mom's room, and placed her key on the table. I went to my room and laid on the bed and cried myself to sleep again. I remembered this happening before in the relationship. I did not sleep long. I woke up the next morning around 7 a.m. I called Andrew, and he answered the phone.

"Where were you at last night, Andrew? I came there and you were not there. It was going on 2 in the morning, Andrew. Really?"

"What are you talking about?" He asked.

"Stop playing with me, Andrew," I said crying. "Why are you playing with me?"

"I was at home," he said.

"You were not at home. Andrew, my car wasn't there." I hung up the phone.

I went to the bathroom and sat on the floor and started crying. I ignored his phone calls for the following days. A week later, I woke up feeling nauseous. I thought about what I ate the night before, and I went on with my day because I had to upload resumes online for a job. It was a fight in me to stay focused and get a job. I did not like going on interviews because I would have to tape the tube to my side so it would not be so noticeable when I would go out in the public and interviews. There were some downfalls with having the tube. That sometimes felt unbearable for me. At times I felt like I could not continue living like this. I was healed but not totally healed yet. I feared, I would have to keep the tube forever. It created a door for the "spirit of fear" to come in, but we know that God did not give me the Spirit of Fear. 2 Timothy 1:7 (NIV) said, *"For God has not given us a spirit of fear and timidity, but of power, love, and self-discipline."*

Even though I had a little shame and fear having the tube, the flip side of having the tube. It was saving my life.

At one point, I used to see it as a reminder of what happened to me. Every day when I looked in the mirror when getting dressed, I cried. A lifetime scar wrapped around my stomach for the rest of my life. Who would want me with this ugly scar? But God! He healed the shame and the embarrassment that I felt. He renewed my mind. Now when I look in the mirror at the scar, it's a constant reminder of who God is to me and how He did not change His mind about me, and to let the devil know who I serve, the God of Abram, Isaac and Jacob.

Maybe your scar is not a physical scar. Maybe it is a scar that people cannot see with the physical eye. Ask God to change how you see your scar. He will do it. Do not look at your scars as something bad, change your perspective. I call it my "Love scars." Maybe it is an internal scar that you long to be healed from. Maybe it is both physical and internal. Great news! God can heal you. God longs to heal all the internal and external hurt.

One day while sitting at home. A week or two later, I got a text from Andrew. "Come to Tallahassee I need to talk to you," he texted. I called him.

"What do we have to talk about, Andrew?" I ask.

"What are you talking about Caroline?" He asked.

"Who are you seeing besides me, Andrew?"

"What? I don't have time to see nobody"

"Where were you that night, Andrew?"

"Okay, I had to go stay at my baby mother's house with my son. His mom had to go to the hospital. I had to stay with him, Carolina."

"Why did you lie when I asked you Andrew?" I asked.

"I knew I could not tell you the truth at the time because you were already mad. Come down here," he said.

With no hesitation, I went. No matter what Andrew told me, I somehow believed him and would be right back into his arms. I took a shower and headed down to Tallahassee. I pulled up to the yard, got out of the car, and went to knock on the screen door. I heard Andrew's voice yelling for me to come in the house.

"It is unlocked. Come in!" He yelled. I walked through the door. "There my baby is, there she is," he said with his arms stretched out for a hug. All the anger that I had built up on the inside of me just instantly went away. I had it on my mind to tell him a thing or too when I saw him. All that went down the drain. With his arms just wrapped around me felt good at the time. He and I kissed and hugged all the way to the bedroom. Of course, he and I had sexual relations. But while we were having sex, his phone kept ringing back-to-back. Once we finished, I asked him, "Who was that calling you back-to-back like that Andrew?"

"I don't know," he said.

I wanted to spend the night, but I knew I could not because my mom was expecting her car back. I went to the bathroom, washed up, and left. I was ready to get my car back so I could start spending the night again. I came out of the bathroom, and I did not see Andrew in the house. I walked outside and saw Andrew on the phone. I felt like being petty and nosey.

What My "Yes" Cost Me

I walked up to him, "Hey, what are you fixing to do?" I asked. Just in case it was another female he was talking to on the phone, she would hear my voice in the background.

"Nothing", he said.

"Why did you rush off the phone when I came outside?"

"Man don't start Caroline. Don't start that tripping. We started off good," he said. (Laughing)

"Whatever Andrew, don't you start. I'm fixing to go home," I said.

"Okay, are you coming back?" He asked.

"No, why you ask me that?"

"I just asked, call me once you make home," he said.

"Okay," I said. We kissed, and I left heading back to my mom's house.

CHAPTER 14

Override the Knowing

I made it back home, took my shoes off, and walk to the bedroom. I called Andrew to let him know I made it back home safely, like he asked, no answer. I waited 10-20 minutes and called back. Still, no answer. I sent a text message. "Hey, pick up the phone. I made it back home." Two hours later, still no text back. I started thinking. Is that why he asked me am I coming back? Naw, I am tripping like Andrew said. It is me, not him. It's me being so clingy. It's all me. I felt like my mind was playing tricks on me at times as Andrew told me. But it was a knowing on the inside of me without having any evidence to prove what I was feeling. It was getting late. I decided to call before I went to bed. Still got no answer from him. My heart just dropped. I wanted to jump up and go there, but I was a little afraid of what I was going to see. I turned over and went to sleep. The next morning, I was awakening by a phone call from Andrew. I picked up the phone.

"Hello," I said.

"Hey, Babe. I saw that you called. I intended to call you back, but I went to sleep."

I held the phone to my ear. I did not know what to believe. Apart of me felt a sense of relief to hear him tell me that but another apart of me would not allow me to believe him. However, I felt I had to believe him because I did not go there to prove to him that he was telling a lie.

"Hello, hello," he said.

"I'm here."

"Did you hear me?" He asked.

"Yeah. I'll call you back Andrew," I said and hung up the phone.

I knew he was lying to me. I could feel it. I was fed up. I felt stupid, hurt, all of the above. I started trying to figure out a way to prove Andrew was lying to me. One morning, I decided when I dropped my mom off at work, I would ride down to Tallahassee just to see what Mr. Andrew had going on. I knew that he would be up that time of the morning. I hoped I had not passed him on the highway heading there. I made it to Tallahassee, and I decide not to go by the house first. I decide to ride down the street then, make my way to his house. I saw my car coming up the street. Geesh! I pulled up on the side of the driver side. I let down the driver side window, and he let the driver side window down. I saw a guy in the passenger seat.

"What's up?" He asked.

I quickly had to come up with something. "Oh nothing," I said.

He nodded his head up and down. "Okay what did you find?" He asked.

"What are you talking about?" I asked.

"Meet me at the house, let me drop him off and I'll be there," he said.

"Okay."

I drove back to the house, sat there, and waiting on him to come. While I was waiting on him, I felt crazy! Like maybe I should not have come down. Minutes later, he pulled up in the yard. I got out the car and headed in the house behind him.

"What's up, Carolina?" He asked.

"What's up, Andrew?"

"What are you fixing to do?" He asked.

"Nothing," I said.

"Come ride with me."

"Okay," I said. We get in my car.

"Where are we going, Andrew?" I asked.

"I'm fixing to show you the neighborhood I want us to stay in."

We rode to the gas station in a small town called English. He started driving through some back roads. I had no clue where we were. All I knew, I was happy to hear that we were moving forward in the right direction in the relationship, and we were together. As we were riding down the highway, I looked out of the window at the sun shining off the bean fields on each side of the highway. It was beautiful. Staying in the deep part of the country town, there was nothing like seeing the sunrise in the morning looking over cotton fields, or bean fields. It is a beautiful sight to see if you enjoy country living. It reminded me when my mom would take my sister and me to see our grandma, riding down U.S. Route 49. We would be looking out the window as little girls asking mom questions about the cotton in the fields. My mind snapped back from reminiscing.

"Andrew, where is this home?" I asked.

"We're almost there, Babe," he said.

We later pulled up to this gated community that you needed a code to get in. The homes were so beautiful. "Wow!" I said. I was wondering where he had gotten a code from, but I knew he did constructional work at times.

"Babe, you like these homes?" He asked.

"Yes, I love these homes," I said.

"This is what I'm going to put you in, Babe, when I get that building up and going. We got to get some more things in place first, Babe."

This is the moment to ask the questions, "When are we going to get married, Andrew? I'm ready for a family," I said.

"We are, Babe. Let's just get this building up and going first, Babe."

After riding around for some hours looking at homes, discussing our future, "I'm hungry, are you?" He asked. "Yeah," I said.

I felt so happy and excited about our future together. His phone rang, and he looked over at me. He picked up the phone and was telling somebody that he was heading back that way in a minute then he hung up the phone. We got something quick to eat and headed back to Tallahassee. Time was getting close for me to pick my mom up from work anyway. We made it back to Tallahassee. I had enough time to eat and head back to pick up mom. I gave him a kiss. "Pick up your phone," I said.

"Okay," he said.

I made it to my mom's job. While I was sitting in the car waiting, I called Andrew and he picked up the phone.

CHAPTER 15

Evidence vs. Him

Andrew and I was finishing our conversation where we left off while I was still waiting on my mom to get off work. Andrew asked the one question I did not like for him to bring up.

"Have y'all came up with amount of how much y'all going are to sue them for?" He asked.

"No, we are not sure how much," I said.

"Don't let them sell you short, Babe," he said.

"Okay."

"I'm not trying to tell you what to do."

"Okay. I'll call you when I make it home," I said.

"Okay."

I remembered my mom telling me not to tell him how much I was getting back from the injury settlement. Mom came out the building and got in the car, and we headed home. All the way home, I was thinking about those beautiful homes Andrew took me to see today. Mom and I made it home. We stopped by the mailbox. We made it inside the apartment. Mom went through the mail and handed me my mail. I had a letter from the doctor's office about my next appointment and another letter from the attorney's office. I was not sure what was inside the letter from my attorney. It had been a back-and-forth thing with the other attorneys. We were getting a lot of kick back from the other end of this settlement.

"Mom, do you mind opening it up to see what they were talking about for me please?"

"Yes," she said. I walked back to the bedroom. She came in the room. "They want to set up a telephone conference with you next week," she said.

"Thanks, Mom," I said.

"You're welcome." She handed me the letter, and I called to set up a conference call with my attorney.

After setting up the conference call with the attorney, I went in my mom's room to talk with her about what was going on with Andrew and me. My mom was not a fan of Andrew. She believed that he was not a good fit for me at all. Especially after this accident that just happened to me. She had her eyes on him closely because of the large sum of money that was involved. I tried to take notice of the warning, and the advice she was giving me. I felt that he was a great fit for me. We were just going through relationship problems as any other relationship. I believed that everything was going to be fine in the relationship. But my mom, family, and friends saw differently.

Sometimes certain people can see things on the outside that you are totally unaware of or blinded by when you are in the relationship. Sometimes it is best to step back and take a full observation of what is taking place on inside and on the outside of the relationship.

The following week came for me to have this conference call with my attorney. My mom and I was out and about taking care of things and getting things for the house. While my mom was in the store, the attorney called me. I was a little excited after the phone call because we were close to closing the settlement. I could not wait to tell my mom the good news about what the attorney told me. Ten minutes later, I got an unusual phone call from a number that had the same prefix number as Andrew. I figured he was calling me from a different phone.

"Hello," I said, and it was a lady voice on the other end of the phone. It felt like a Barbara vs. Shirley moment. I can laugh about it now, but it was not funny then.

"Hello," she said.

"Hello."

"Who is this?" She asked.

"Who are you? You called my number."

"I'm trying to see who is calling my man's number," she said.

"Who is your man?" I asked. "This is Carolina. Who are you?"

"I'm Ann," she said.

"Who is your man again? You did not say."

"Andrew," she said.

"What?"

"B****, you need to stop calling him!" she stated. She went on to say if I did not stop seeing her man and calling him, what all she was going to do to me. Before I could get a word in, she had hung up the phone in my face. I called back, and it went to voicemail. I was so angry.

My mom came back to the car. "What's wrong with you, why are you looking like that?" She asked. "Nothing, mom", I said. I went on to tell her what the attorney said. She still knew something was up with me.

I could not wait to ask mom to use her car. "Mom, can I use your car for a second?" I asked. "Yeah," she said.

I could not make it to Tallahassee fast enough to see what this lady was talking about. I dropped mom off, and I headed down to Tallahassee. I was replaying everything she was saying, I was pushing the pedal down a little bit more. I pulled out my phone to call Andrew, but his phone went to voicemail. That made it worse. I did not care about him not picking up the phone. I was on my way there to see what was going on. Have you ever been in a hurry to get to a place to find out that no matter how fast you drove, the outcome was still going to be same even if you drove the speed limit, especially in my case? I made it safely to his house. I saw my car parked in the front yard. I jumped out the car. I had the door open before I put the car in park. A Flintstone moment. I did not knock on the door. The screen door was unlocked. I walked in and turned the knob on the front door of the house, but it was lock. I knocked hard on the door, and Andrew comes and open the door.

"Andrew, who in the hell is Ann?" I asked.

"Who?" he asked.

"WHO IS, Ann? Why did she call me saying stay away from her man?" I showed him the phone number.

"Man, that lady's just jealous of you because I told her I wanted to be with you and not her", he said.

"LIAR, call her now, Andrew," I said. "I'm not playing with you, CALL HER!" He pulled out his phone, and he called her.

"Put the phone on speaker, Andrew," I demanded. The phone started ringing, and she picked up the phone.

"Man, why are you calling my woman telling her that I am your man? You know I told you I did not want you Ann," he said. She started yelling through the phone. He hung up the phone before she could get anything out.

"Who is she, Andrew?" I asked.

"She's just somebody that stays down the street that like me," he said. "She like a bad disease I cannot get rid of."

"What! Are you sleeping with this lady, Andrew?" I asked.

"Not anymore, I used to sleep with her," he said.

"When?" I asked.

"Long before I met you," he said.

"Are you still sleeping with this lady now, when I am not down here?" I asked.

"HELL NO," he said.

"Let's go down to her house," I said.

"No, we are not going down to that lady house," he said. "You have a tube hanging out of your stomach. Sit down and calm down Carolina.

"What does that mean?" I asked.

"That lady is a nobody to me," he said. So, he and I went on and on about the lady. Until I got tired of asking the questions. That day I was demanding answers. I was not going anywhere until I felt like he answered all the questions. It was a boldness that came over me. But not enough to leave him alone. Needless, to say, I was not mindful that I had a tube in my stomach, one wrong move would have mess me up. Andrew had me totally convinced that this lady was just a troublemaker, and she just wanted to mess up our relationship, and that it was not him, it was her.

You may be in a wrong relationship right now where things just do not add up? And you know it and you are fighting against holding on to the relationship or letting go. Do not have "Autoimmune Mindset Spirit" in the relationship, meaning fighting against what's in your mind and heart. When the evidence in plain eyesight. Do not ignore the evidence.

CHAPTER 16

He was the Drug, and I Was the Addict

After all of that going back and forth with Andrew about Ann. I was still not satisfied with the situation. When Andrew was not in my presence, I would think to myself, was Ann really telling me the truth or a lie? Then, I thought about the times when he was not picking up the phone. Was he with Ann? The thought of her staying down the street from him and them both living in the same small town. That just intensified my feelings that I was already feeling and my mind even more. When I would go down to see him, I never wanted to leave because I knew Ann stayed a lot closer to Andrew than me. I stayed 30 minutes away from him when she had advantage over me staying two minutes away. I started to go down there a lot more. One day while sitting at home, my nursing colleague, Lynn, called and invited me out to lunch with her. I was all for it because with the recent drama I had with Andrew, I needed to get out. Anyone that ever had any dealings with me knew how I felt about Andrew. I tried hard not to focus on Andrew while we were out. It was crazy because I was with her physical eating out, but mentally, I was not there at all. I could not stand the thought of that because I felt like it was robbing me of my joy and precious moments with family, friends.

Have you ever been going through something, and you tried to do everything you could to shift your mind off what you were going through? But your situation robbed you of your moment with loved ones. Do not allow your circumstances to take away your joy of the present moment. Go get ice cream or do something that is going to bring you happiness. With me everything was about Andrew. My life became consumed with him. My mind, body and soul. Having ungodly soul ties with the wrong person will make you think you are in love. When in fact it is "False Love." It causes a sense of delusion.

I was still with Andrew and at this point, I knew he was no good for me. I cannot figure out why I was still with him? I woke up with him on my mind. I went to sleep thinking about him. It felt like he was the drug, and I was the addict. It feels like I was enslaved mentally, soul, and body to him. Let the truth be told, no one, but God is supposed to be on your mind that much. You are not supposed to feel burden down. According to Romans 8:5-7, *"Those who live according to the flesh have their minds set on what the flesh desires. The mind governed by the flesh is death, but the mind governed by the Spirit is life. The mind governed by the flesh is hostile to God; it does not submit to God's law, nor can it do so."* Does your relationship feel like life or death? You are supposed feel free and full of life. Every relationship has good and bad. That goes for business or personal. But not a heavy burden that you can't bear. You should have joy, peace, and love in the relationship. Your thoughts should be making sure you are doing the will of your Father. Do not get me wrong, I am not saying do not love your spouse, or your loved ones. There is big difference between the two. It should never be to the point that an individual has that type of power over your mind, body and soul. Where it feels like you are addicted to that person. If you are displaying this type of behavior in the relationship right now, you might want to analyze it. That is bondage, and enslavement to your mind, body and soul. And you need to be set free.

Many months later, Andrew and I relationship turned for the worse. I tried to stay positive focused on what was ahead. I felt addicted to something that was getting worse, but I could not escape from it. As things began to grow and intensify in our relationship. I began to go to Tallahassee during the late nights just to see if Andrew would be at home like he told me. Two in the morning, I got my mom's keys to the car, and I drove down to Tallahassee. I did not call him, nor did I text him because he told me that he was at home, and he was getting ready to go to bed. As I was driving to his house, a funny feeling came in my belly. A part of me wanted to find out, but a part of me did not. I made it to his house. I pulled up, and I did not see my car in the front yard. Immediately!! This again! When I did not see my car in the front or the back yard and all the lights were out in the house, my mind immediately went to Ann. I remembered Andrew saying that she stayed in Tallahassee down the street. I was not sure where she stayed, but Tallahassee was small town. I drove down every street until I saw my car just when I was about to give up on looking. I turned down a street, and I saw my car parked in a driveway pulled up at a house behind a vehicle. I pulled up in the driveway. I knew my tag number to my car. Sure, enough it was my car. My first thought was what if I get into a fight? Was I really prepared to fight? *Never allow anger rule over you.* I got out the car anyway. I did not have anything to protect myself with other than my fist. I was prepared to use them. I walked up to the door. I knocked on the screen door. I saw a light come on.

What My "Yes" Cost Me

A woman voice yelled, "Who is it?"

"Where is Andrew, tell him to come outside," I said. The door had opened.

"He's not here," she said. Her voice sounded so familiar, but I was not focused on that.

"Yes, he is. That's my car in your driveway," I said.

"No, he is not here," she said. I walked back to the car and drove off so angry. I wanted to bust through her door and walk through the house until I found him. I knew she was lying to me. Who is she? I thought driving back home. I was angry, hurt, confused, and embarrassed. How could he drive my car to another woman's house and sitting in her house? And hear me at the door and not come out the house? Are you serious, Andrew? I yelled out hitting the steer wheel. How could you do this to me, Andrew? I hate you, Andrew. I made up in my mind that was it! I am picking up my car tomorrow. I will take my chance on the repo people picking up the car. I'd rather have that than to have him laying up with another woman with my car. I could not wait until day light hit. I needed to get my car. The next morning, I called my cousin Tammy and told her what happened. She was shocked but not really because she knew Andrew's behavior. Tammy and I put our plan to work. I asked her if I were to drive my mom's car there, would drive it back while I drove my car back. She agreed to plan.

CHAPTER 17

When the Plan Goes Wrong

That morning, my cousin, Tammy came over to my mom's place. We sat down at the kitchen isle, and we started laughing and cracking jokes. When I spoke with her on the phone, I asked her would she come in the morning so we could ride down to Tallahassee to pick up my car up and quickly come back before Andrew got moving around. As we were sitting in the kitchen after a couple of minutes, we put the plan into motion. I asked my mom if I could use the car for a second. "Yes," she said. "Thanks, mom," I responded. "Come on Tammy. Are you ready?" I asked. We left headed down to Tallahassee to give Andrew a piece of my mind and take my car back. As we were riding down, we put on some music to get us hyped up. We talked about how we were going to get the car. We made it down to Tallahassee. We pulled up to the yard, but my car was not in the yard again. I still went to the screen door and knocked. He did not answer door. We left his house and rode over the lady's house where my car was last night. My car was not there either. I called Andrew to see where he was with my car. I did not want to give off any clue to him that I was coming to pick up the car. He picked up the phone.

"Hello," he said.

"Where are you?" I asked.

"I'm in Gart town," he said.

"I want my car back, Andrew." I could not hide it any longer that I wanted my car back. We started driving towards Stuttgart to see if I would pass him on the highway. "Where are you in Gart?" I asked.

"Why?" He asked.

"I need my car." I hung the phone up.

"What did he say?" Tammy asked. I knew I had blown the plan.

"He's in Gart town. Maybe we will see him on the highway coming back this way."

"Is he going to give your car back? What is wrong with him?" She asked.

"I don't know," I said. We let the windows down and turned the music up and headed towards Gart town. I was not sure if he was lying about where he was just to throw me off. We made to Gart, I called him. He did not pick up the phone. I called him again, and he answered.

"Where are you in Gart? I'm here. Where is my car, Andrew? Stop playing with me," I said. My cousin, Tammy, and I pulled into a gas station to put gas in mom's car. I hit the button to roll the driver side window up, but the window would not let up.

"Oh, my goodness. Why is the window not letting up, Tammy?" I asked.

"What? Really?" She asked.

"Yes. Can you go pay for the gas while I try to get this window up?" I asked.

"Yeah," she said.

I pumped the gas. We got in the car, and the window still did not let up. How am I going to explain this to my mom? Was this a sign for me to just let him keep the car, and we head back home?

"What is going on?" Tammy asked.

"I don't know, Tammy," I said. We both looked at each other and busted out and laughing. That is all we could do at the time. We pulled over at this shop to see if these guys could help us get the driver's side window up. They could not help us. My goodness how in the world am I going to be able to explain this to my mom. It was no longer a priority for me to get my car back. It was getting my mom's driver window up before making it back home. All the way back home my cousin,

Tammy, and I tried to come up with excuses as to why the window did not let up.

"My goodness. Aunt Tiny's not going to take this too well," she said.

"I know she's not," I said. We both started giggling. Laughing about how we thought we had a plan, and it went left. We pulled up in the parking lot. We sat in the car dreading going upstairs telling my mom what happened.

"Let me try to let the window up one more time," I said. "TAMMY!!!" I yelled. "It went up. Yessss!!!" I was so excited that the window went up. Right on time! Afterwards I still wanted my car back. I was not done with Andrew yet! Tammy left quickly after that. I called Andrew, he picked up.

"Andrew how in the h*** you going to have my car over another woman house?" I asked.

"What are you talking about?"

"You know what I'm talking about," I said.

"I was not over another woman's house last night."

"Look that's it! I'm done with you, just bring me my car. You are not going to tell the truth, just bring me my CAR!" I yelled.

"Look I was not over, but your car was at her house. I let her son use your car," he said.

"WHATTTT!!" I yelled. "Who is she?"

"Ann," he said.

"WHATT?? I knew her voice sounded familiar", I said. "Have you lost your mind, Andrew? How are you going to let her son use my car? You have lost your mind, Andrew."

"I'll drop your car off in the morning. You are wrong," he said. "I was not in that lady's house."

"If you were not in her house then where were you?" I asked.

"I was over a homeboy's house of mind," he said.

"Andrew, you were in that house. I'm done with you. Just drop my car like you said you were going to do, and we are done," I said.

"Okay," he said.

The next morning, I had gotten up early, waiting on Andrew to bring me the car. A knock on the door.

"Who is it?" I asked.

"It's me! Open up the door." I knew Andrew's voice. I opened the door he started kissing on me.

"Stop," I said. "Don't kiss on me. I don't know where your lips have been.

"Come drop me off back in Tallahassee since you want your car back, but before you do, gimme some," he said.

"What? You got me messed up. I'm done with you, Andrew."

"I'm telling you the truth. Her son needed a way to work so I let him borrow the car," he said.

"I'll drop you off in Tallahassee. Let me get myself together," I said. He went and sat down in the living room until I finished getting dress. Once I finished getting dress we headed to Tallahassee.

"Andrew, I cannot believe you let her son use my car. Why did you do that?" I asked. He looked at me with a blank stare.

"I don't know," he said.

"You had my car over that lady's house who called me on my phone and told me that you were her man. Are you serious, Andrew?" I asked. "How could you do something like that to me?" I asked again. I had one hand on the steering wheel and just started hitting him with the other.

"Heyy! STOP! You're tripping for no reason," he said. "Just let me out right here. I will call somebody else to take me back to Tallahassee," he said.

"She is a nobody right? Then let's go to her house together and get this straight right now," I said.

"I'm not going over nobody's house," he said. We went back and forth all the way to Tallahassee. Once we made it to Tallahassee, I drove passed the street where his house was.

"Stop don't go to that woman's house starting nothing, Carolina," he said.

"No, you started it when you had my car over her house. She started it by calling my phone with the foolishness.

"I'm telling you, don't go over her house," he said. "The boy needed a way to work."

"Who are you to figure out a way for him to get to work?" I asked. I turned the car around and we headed back over his house. We got out the car and went inside his house.

"Andrew let's call her," I said.

"I don't know why you wish to go back and forth with somebody. She is silly and going to tell you what you want to hear," he said. "Come on." He grabbed and pulled me into the bedroom by the hand.

"Andrew, this doesn't solve our problems," I said. "No!"

"Okay," he said.

"I'm getting ready to leave," I said. I left and headed back to the house.

Some days had passed. Andrew and I still texted each other back and forth. In between the text messages. Andrew and I agreed to get back together. I said "Yes to he and I getting back together. I felt committed and addicted to a dysfunctional YES relationship! One day Andrew texted me, "Just to let you know one of my baby mothers let me use one of cars, since you took your car back." "I want to go ahead and tell you". He said. He thought that was going to rattle me, but it did not. I was not happy about it, but I was okay with it. I knew I was not going to allow him back in my car after seeing my car parked at Ann's house. I still had it on my mind to call Ann. I just had not figured out when, but I wanted to hear her side of the story.

CHAPTER 18

Ann's Story

Finally, I called Ann. Despite what Andrew was telling me about her. I got his side of the story. How much he loves me and how sorry he was for hurting me, and that we had a bright future ahead of us. The thought was still hanging over my head to find out Ann's side of the story. Andrew did not want me to go to her house, nor did he want me to call her. He told me that if I called her, I would be wasting my time. She wanted to destroy what he and I had going on, and she was a lady that just could not let him go. He wanted me to leave the past in the past and focus on what he and I was building together.

Andrew and I was still seeing each other after the big blow up about Ann and my car being at her house.

Something in me just would not let that rest about the Ann situation. I decided to give Ann a call one day. I called the number back she called me from. She picked up the phone.

"Hello, is this Ann?" I asked.

"Yeah," she said.

"This is Andrew's girlfriend, Carolina," the one you called the other day.

"Yeah," she said.

"I am calling to find out what is going because I feel like Andrew is not telling me the truth about some things. Can you tell me why my car was at your house the other night? Was he in your house?" I asked.

"You have to ask him that," she said.

"What? I'm asking you. What is going on between you and Andrew?" I asked.

"Andrew and I have been seeing each for some years now, off and on. He comes over every other night.

I cook, clean his house, and wash his clothes for him," she said.

"Okay," I said. Holding back what I really wanted to say. I hung up the phone.

All along what I felt in my belly was now coming to pass. I had the evidence to prove what I was feeling on the inside. I could not hear any more of what she had to say. I thought about all the nights I was not with him. I called Andrew and told him what Ann just shared with me. I did not give him time to sweet talk his way out of it. I hung up the phone on him. I changed my number and was done with him. Words could not describe what I was feeling. I tried to move on with my life. Then I thought, maybe she was lying about what was going between them like Andrew said, she would do anything to keep him to herself. All the maybes popped up in my mind. All I knew was I was missing Andrew. I was torn between her telling me her side of the story, and Andrew telling his side of the story. I have known different type of females would tell a lie just to see the relationship fall.

A month later, I called Andrew from my new number. I could not hold back any longer. I wanted to hear his voice. I had defeated the whole purpose of me changing my number. *There are times it may be hard to break away from something you said "YES" to or someone you are comfortable or familiar with. Don't allow your "YES" to cost your sanity like it did me.* He picked up the phone.

"Hello," he said.

"What are you doing Andrew?" I asked.

"Nothing, what have you been up to?" He asked. I could hear the excitement in his voice. I think we both were excited to hear each other's voice.

"Nothing," I said.

"I cannot believe you took that woman's word over what I told you, "he said. I did not say anything. I held the phone to my ear.

"I miss you," he said.

"I miss you, too." We started talking all over again.

The following week I had to meet with my attorney and the mediator. They told me and my mom that things were flowing good with the settlement. Later that day, I called Andrew to see if he had any plans for the night. I told him I might come to see him. He said that he had to run to a couple of places and once he made it back home, he would give me a call. Before he and I got off the phone, Andrew expressed to me how much he was thinking about me and missed me so deeply. Andrew knew the right words to say to me and the right things to do. That would lead me right back into his arms. It was as if Andrew had studied me, it felt like Andrew knew me better than I knew myself which was dangerous. When Andrew called me back a couple of hours later and told me that tonight was not a good night for him because he was tired, I did not go back and forth with him. I agreed with him since we had just started back talking to each other, and it had been a month since he and I had been around each other.

I waited until midnight and headed to Tallahassee. I was not going to stop at his house. I just wanted to see if someone else was at his house. Well, I made to Tallahassee, I rode passed the street were Andrew lived. I turned around and made a circle and came back on the street where he lived. I saw a car in the yard. I assumed that was the baby mother's car that he told me a month ago before he and I stopped talking. I wanted to see if he was at home or not. I knew what our past arguments would consist of. I got back on the highway and went home. When I made it home, I got in the shower and went to sleep.

I was doing things that what was not in my character in this relationship. I was turning into someone I would not have ever dreamt of becoming.

CHAPTER 19

Shattered Dreams

I woke up to my mom coming into my room.

Carolina, where is your car?" I thought I was dreaming. I had to just lay in bed for a minute and think about it. I wanted to say Andrew had my car. I jumped up from the bed and ran to the living room window. I did not see my car outside.

"Oh, my goodness," I said. "Mom, did someone steal my car?" Then I thought about. I believed my car was repossessed. I remembered what time I made it back home in the car last night. They must have picked the car up shortly after I made it home. I called to find out where my car was so I could get some my personal things out of it. I found the car and mom took me to get my things. On our way back home, I felt somewhat sad about my car getting repossessed, but I knew I could not afford to pay the car payments. I had not found a nursing job and was in middle of a legal lawsuit. I felt like everything was shattered. What was the point of going to college if it was going to be this hard getting a job? The jobs kept saying you needed experience. It felt pointless. I couldn't catch a break.

Sometimes when you are going through life it comes to a point, where it seems as if you are losing/lost everything around and you have no control of it. Dreams shattered! It may seem as if everything around you is shattered. God will restore to you DOUBLE! Do not fret! I want you to be inspired. Better days is coming your way. Joel 2: 25-32, *"I'll make up for the years of the locust."* God will restore what you have lost.

A thought came to my mind that maybe I should have left my car with Andrew. Once mom and I made it back home, I went in the room, put my stuff that I had gathered out the car on the floor, laid down on the bed, and I started thinking. It felt like I was losing everything close to me. I did not understand it at all. I felt so miserable inside and outside. I had nothing but a nurse's license that I could not use. I felt limited. "Do not give up, Carolina," mom said. If you are reading this and you feel like you are hitting a brick wall in your business, career, ministry, etc., do not give up because on the other side of that wall is a big blessing assigned with your name on it. She told me you will find a job in the nursing field. My mom was my biggest supporter, and my biggest fan. She would encourage me every time she felt I was getting depressed about anything, and guess what? She was right.

My mom would also tell me when I would be wrong about things. Especially when it came to Andrew. My mom had her radar on when it came to him. It even got to the point where my mom did not want me driving her car down to Tallahassee anymore. I had to tell her sometimes that I would be going to the store, and I would be right back, but I would go to Tallahassee to see Andrew. But with my mom, you could not pull too many things over on her. I told

Andrew the news about the car getting picked up from mom place, but he really did not have too much to say about it which I figured. He told me that he was here for me if I needed anything. I knew what he meant when he would say that. When it was convenient for Andrew, he would give me money.

I remembered Andrew helped me get my new braces on my teeth. At the time, I was working for the Department of Correction and the benefits did not cover the full amount. I knew at time his help came with conditions. With my mom and I having to share one car, I still needed to get back and forth to my liver specialist. My mom was doing all she could to help us both. I asked Andrew if he would take me sometimes to my doctor's appointment, and he agreed to it. He would pick me up in his baby mother's car and take me to the doctor's appointment. That felt awkward riding around in one of his kid's mother's vehicles. Andrew knew I felt uncomfortable riding in her car. I addressed concerns to him. What choice did I have at the time? None! He told me not to worry about the small stuff.

"Caroline, you got to get to these doctor's appointment babe," he said.

"You are right," I said. Afterwards we would stop and get something to eat after every doctor's appointment.

I started back spending the night at his house. One weekend, I spent with Andrew, we had a good time that weekend. He and I went to pick up some things for the building that he had started working on. He always said he wanted to turn that building into a bar and grill place.

"See Babe, I don't have time to be running around on you, I'm trying to get this building up and running for us," he said. I knew Andrew had 18-wheeler trucks on the highway along with other little side businesses, but he would always assure me that his hard work was for me, kids' and him. And that it was no way he had time to be cheating on me. "I'm thinking about naming the building after my little girl," he said.

"Oh, that would be nice, Andrew," I said. I knew he loved his kids. I said to myself, "Andrew is right. I am tripping for no reason. He loves me and the kids."

CHAPTER 20

Holding On To Dysfunction

I was awakened to bright, sun, shining through the bedroom blinds. I turned over and reached for my phone. I saw a text from Andrew, "I love you". I texted back, "Love you too." Andrew told me he had gotten me something. Andrew surprised me with a Big 65-inch TV. Andrew and Bill brought the TV to my mom's house and set it up for me. After setting up the TV, Andrew asked me did I need anything else. I told him no I was good. I thanked him for the TV. He, then, gave me some money in my hands and gave me a kiss. It would be moments like that I wanted to hold on to and not let go of.

A week later, I got up out of the bed and went to the bathroom to brush my teeth. I heard the phone ringing from the kitchen. I forgot I left the phone plugged up in the kitchen the prior night. By the time I had finished brushing my teeth and ran in the kitchen to pick it up, it stopped ringing. A missed called from nursing colleague, Lynn. It was that time again. Once a month, she would come up to the city to do some shopping and we would go out to eat. I called her back.

"Hey, Carolina what you doing? I'm here in your city," she said.

"Okay, let's go get something to eat girl," I said.

"Okay, come ride with me to the store first, then we can go eat. I'm right down the street from you."

I was always excited to see Lynn. There was a knock at the door.

"Who is it?" I asked.

"It's Lynn!"

"Come in," I said. "Let me finish getting dressed and grab my purse, and then I will be ready."

"Okay," she said. Minutes later we headed out the door.

"What is going on with you and Andrew? Are you still seeing him?" She asked once we got in the car.

"Same thing, girl. Nothing has changed," I said.

"Has he changed any since the last time we talked?" She asked.

"Not really, Lynn," I said.

"When are y'all going to get married?" She asked.

"I don't know, girl," I said. "That's the same thing I want to know. He said he wanted to wait until this building up and running.

"What building?" She asked.

"Girl, he has a building he is working on down in Tallahassee that he is trying to turn into Bar and Grill," I said.

"Okay, that sounds nice," she said. "Where are we going to eat at this time?" She asked. We love eating pizza. We went and ate at this great pizza and salad place. While we were eating, I texted Andrew.

"What are you doing?"

"Working," he texted back.

After we finished eating, I began to feel nauseous again. Sometimes I would feel a little nauseous due to the injury I had. It was not unusual for me to feel nausea.

"Girl, I feel so nauseous," I said.

"You pregnant? "She asked.

"No ma'am," I said.

Lynn dropped me back off at the apartment after we finished eating. I laid down for a few minutes. Moments later, I jumped up and ran to the bathroom. I began to vomit everything I had just finished eating. It was different for me to vomit. I cleaned myself up, gargled, and rinsed my mouth out. I sat down on the side of the bed to get myself together. It was getting close for my mom to make it home from work. I was still trying to figure out why I just vomited. In my mind, I began to think about when my last cycle was. Mom made it home from work. I waited until mom got settled in from work before just jumping into a conversation about my day. I walked into my mom's room.

"Hey mom! How was your day?" I asked.

"It was okay," she said.

"Do you want me to go and get you something to eat mom?" I asked.

"I'm going to cook my zucchini, squash, and sausage," she said. My mom loved her zucchini and squash.

"Okay," I said. "Mom, guess what happen to me today?

"What?" She asked.

"Lynn came to Little Rock today, and we went out to eat pizza, and I started feeling nauseous," I said.

"Well Carolina, you know the doctor told you that you might feel like that sometimes," she said.

"No Mom. I vomited everything I ate," I said.

"The food may have not sat well with you today," she said.

"Yeah Mom, you are right." I said. I was so relieved. I knew if my mom said it, it was true. She had two kids of her own. "Mom, can I use the car to go see Andrew?" I asked. She gave me a look that people would say would kill.

"You know I don't like you going down there. Go ahead, and don't be there long. I got to go to work in the morning," she said. I called Andrew just to see was he home.

"Hello," he said.

"Hey, you at home?" I asked.

"No, I'm in Monroe working on this truck," he said.

"Oh okay," I said.

"Let me call you back," he said.

"Okay," I said. I took the keys back in the room to my mom.

"What happened?" She asked.

"He is not at home," I said.

"I wish you would leave him alone, Carolina," she said.

As crazy as this may sound, sometimes you feel like it is better to hold on to dysfunctional rather than to let go. You do not have to be in something that is dysfunctional to comfort your flesh. Don't allow yourself to be so entangle in dysfunction. The enemy might tell you there is nobody else better out there for you. If you let, go of what you are gripping so tight too. Your wrong "Yes" will cause you start to tolerate and put with things you usually would not tolerate or put up with in life or in a relationship.

CHAPTER 21

Acceptance Phase

It was midnight. I woke up to a text message. I was excited, I knew it was Andrew, asking me to come and see him, but this number I did not recognize. I opened the text message, and it was an inappropriate picture of another female. I texted back wrong number. They texted back, "No it's not." I sat up in the bed and called the number.

"Hello," I said.

A female voice answered, "B****, leave my man alone. He doesn't want you," she said, and hung the phone up in my face.

I sat up on the side of the bed and said to myself, another female. I tried to call the number back. It went to voicemail. It did not sound like Ann's voice. This female's voice was a little deeper than Ann's. I called Andrew's phone. The first ring went straight to his voicemail. I tried to go back to sleep, but I could not sleep. I called Andrew again. Back to his voicemail. I remember saying, "Really?". I decided to put my clothes on, I knew Mom was sleeping. I grabbed the keys to the car. There I was, heading down to Tallahassee. We had just finished going through this. Why would Andrew give another woman my number? And to top it off, to have her to send me an inappropriate picture. I made it to Tallahassee. I pulled up to Andrew's house. The porch light was on. No vehicle was in the yard. I did not get out the car. I sat in the car and just thought, okay if he's not at home. Then where could he be? He must be at Ann's house. I drove down the street. I did not pull up in the driveway but pulled back out because I did not see the vehicle Andrew had been driving. But that meant nothing when it came to Andrew.

The hunt began. Where could he be this time of night? If he was not at Ann's house. Where does this other woman live? Not knowing where to start. After puzzling my brain, I began to accept the fact that if he was not going to be with me, then he is with Ann…now, another woman. I headed back home wondering, where could he be? I tried to think positive. Maybe he had to be with his son. Never in a million years had I thought I would accept any man cheating on me. I did not tolerate this in my first marriage, which ended in a divorce. Why am I accepting this from him? That was the million-dollar question. I made it back home. I was drained mentally. It was at the point that I started accepting the fact that when Andrew did not answer his phone at nights for me, I knew he would turn his phone back on in the morning, and I would hear from him then, and I was okay with that. I began to accept anything from him. I even began to accept the words that came out of his mouth. Despite what I knew and saw with my own eyes. I must be honest. The more he and I began to draw closer to each other, the worse it got.

The next morning, I called his phone. It was to the point when I would be happy to hear the phone ring more than twice. I knew his phone was on. He answered the phone.

"Hello," he said.

"Andrew, did you have another female text my phone last night?" It was silent on the other end of the phone.

"Let me call you back," he said.

"No! Answer me," I said. "Did you, or did you not have another female text my phone with a nasty picture, and did you have her to tell me that you did not want me?"

He hung up the phone in my face. I called him back. He picked up the phone.

"Hey, let me call you back, okay?" I hung up the phone. I began to cry. I texted him. I knew he would read my text if he did not want to talk to me on the phone. I texted him.

"Why Andrew would you do that to me? What did I do to you for you to do that to me?" He did not immediately text back. I could not wait until Mom came home from work to go there to confront him. I was not getting anywhere with him on this phone. Three hours had passed. I called him.

"Yeah," he answered.

"Why would you do that to me?" I asked.

"I'm done with you," he said.

"What?" I asked.

"I don't want to be in a relationship with nobody," he said.

"Are you serious Andrew? So, it is true. You did have that female call me and send me that mess," I said.

"I don't want you or her. Yeah, if that's what you want me to say," he said.

"No, I want the truth," I said.

"I got to go, and I don't know what you are talking about," he said. He hung up the phone. I dropped down and began to cry until I could not cry anymore. I laid in the bed. I heard my mom walk in the door.

"Carolina," she called out. She opened my bedroom door. "What's wrong with you? Why are you still in the bed?" She asked. As I continued to stay in the bedroom all day. I could smell my mom cooking. "Carolina, have you eaten today?"

"No not yet," I said. I did not have a taste for any food.

My mom knew something was wrong with me if I was not asking for the car keys to go to Tallahassee to see Andrew, I would be up talking to her. She did not push the issue of asking what was going on with me. It felt as if a bomb was dropped on me. I was stuck in a never-ending cycle.

A month later, no text message or phone call from Andrew. I was not going to reach out to him either. One day while sitting in the living allowing the TV watched me. I was just replaying what Andrew told me on the phone. I took notice that it should be that time of the month for me. For years in my mind, I knew I could not get pregnant. In my first marriage, we tried several times to have a baby. We were unsuccessful. My ex-husband and I went to an OBGYN to see why we could not conceive. The OBGYN said, "Well, I do not know what your religion is but there is nothing keeping you guys from getting pregnant. It is all in God's time," he said. I remembered walking out the doctor's office happy. The big question in our mind was why it has not happened for us yet?

Many times, as people when things don't happen on our time schedule. We immediately go into trying to fix it ourselves. Trying to make it happen. At God appointed time, your prayers will come to pass. Mind blowing blessings. God always give his children his best. For his Glory!

CHAPTER 22

Rejection Phase

A week later, I get a text from Andrew.

"I miss you, Carolina," he texted.

"Yeah, right," I texted back. He had told me this before. To be honest, I was happy when he sent me that text message. I wanted to play hard with him.

"What are you doing?" He texted.

"Nothing," I texted back. "What are you doing?" Then my phone rung.

"Hello," I said.

"I miss you," he said.

"I thought you was done with me," I said.

"I just said that because you were getting on my nerves," he said. "I get tired of arguing with you about females that I am not messing with," he said.

"What? Are you kidding me, Andrew? They call me. Sounds like you are riding in the car or something."

"Yeah, I had to drop something off at my son's school," he said.

"Oh okay. What have you been up to with your new girlfriend?" I asked.

"I'm not with nobody," he said. "I've been throwing up yellow stuff."

"Vomiting?" I asked.

"Yeah," he said. "I been at home sick," he said.

"Are you serious?" I asked.

"Yeah, why?" He asked.

"I vomited once after I ate some pizza sometime back," I said. "I'm waiting on my cycle to come now. I don't know, Andrew."

"I've been throwing up yellow and clear stuff for past couple of days," he said.

"Who did you get pregnant?" I asked.

"I have not been having sex with nobody to get nobody pregnant!"

"Yeah right," I said.

"You were the last person I had sex with," he said.

"Whatever. I don't believe that Andrew," I said. "What about that female that sent me that picture that night?

"I told you that's nothing," he said.

"Okay, Andrew." I would normally ask Andrew to tell me the truth, but I did not feel up to arguing with him.

Another week had passed, and I still had not had a cycle. I took a pregnancy test knowing it would be negative like always. I went to the store to pick up a cheap pregnancy test. I came back home; I went into the restroom and took the test. I went back in the restroom and saw double lines in the window of the stick. I could not believe it, so I started to reread the instructions again. I thought, maybe this pregnancy test was too cheap, and it was reading inaccurate. I will check it again in the morning I know for sure I will get a better reading when my HCG will be higher.

Morning did not come quick enough for me. The next morning, I got up and followed the instructions all the way to correct time. Double lines pop up in the window again on the stick. I was happy to tell my mom. I could not wait to pick mom up from work and tell her the good news. I wanted to wait to tell Andrew. I wanted to confirm it by a OBGYN doctor first. I was not sure how he was going to take the news. Knowing that our relationship was rocky, and we just started back taking again. The joy I felt after telling my mom about the good news felt so great. My mom and I researched for some local OBGYNs in the area. We found an OBGYN that could get me in an early appointment. I had to still wait another 2 weeks before I could see the

OBGYN. Andrew and I kept open communication between us. The day came for me to see the OBGYN. I was a little nervous because I was going by myself. My mom could not take off work; she had exhausted all her time when my injury happened. I remember walking into the doctor's office. The front desk receptionist greeted me with smiles and asked me to sign in. Afterwards, she handed me some forms to fill out. I went back to my seat, and I began to scan through the forms. I ran across the form that asked the question if you knew who the father was to list his name. I was afraid to list his name. Not because I did not know he was the father but because I had not told him about me expecting, and now I had to list his name. Not sure if they were going to contact him or what. Plus, Andrew knew a lot of people everywhere. After I finished filling out the forms, I took the forms back up to the front desk and sat back down. Soon after they called my name to the back. The young lady handed me a urine cup and asked me to give some urine and directed me where the restroom was.

"Once you finish, go to the open door to your right and have a seat," she said. I did as she directed me too. I was still a little nervous. I left the cup in the restroom as directed and walked to the room and sat down.

I looked down at my phone and texted my mom, "I'm here at the doctor's office in the back now. I will call you once I come out."

"Okay," she texted back. The young lady came in took some basic information from me before the doctor came in. She asked me to change into the gown. She told me that she and the doctor would be right in.

CHAPTER 23

Mind Blown Announcement

In November 2010, I am sitting in the room waiting for the doctor and nurse to come in. The doctor came in the room and introduced himself, along with the nurse.

"I looked over your chart," he said. He asked me some more questions. Then, he asked me to lay back on the table. Each step of the way he told me what was going to take place. "Lay back I'm going to do ultrasound," he said. I laid back and he put the gel on my stomach. He began to press down on my belly. "Umm," he said.

"Is everything okay?" I asked.

"Yes, everything," he said.

"Okay," I said. He wiped the gel off my stomach.

"Can you sit up for me?" He asked.

"Tell me a little history of your mom and father background," he stated.

"As far as what, sir?" I asked.

"On your mom's side of the family, does twins run on her side of family?" He asked.

"Umm, I'm not sure," I said. I was trying to run down the family's history of who I knew that is close that is a twin, but before I could answer…

"What about your father? Does he have twins that run in the family?"

I could not think. "I'm not sure," I said.

"Well, you are pregnant, but I see twins!" he said.

"Twins!" I repeated back to him to make sure I heard him correctly.

"Yes, twins! Maybe the children's father has twins on his side of the family," he said.

"I'm pregnant with twins?" I asked again. I was in shock for a second.

"Yes, you are pregnant with twins," he said. He began to give me a list of foods and vitamins he wanted me to take. He told me that he wanted to follow up with me in another 2 weeks. It seemed as if he wanted me to double up on everything. I was glad that he put everything on paper because I was still trying to take in the fact that I was pregnant with twins. I left the office and went to my mom's job. I called her before I went inside of the building to see if it was okay for me come to her office. I called my mom.

"Mom, are you busy?" I asked. "I'm outside. I want to come to the office and talk with you,"

"Yeah, come on up," she said.

This could not wait until she was off work. I walked in the building, signed in, and went to my mom's office. I went to my mom's desk, and she told me to sit down.

"What happened?" She asked.

"Mom, he said that I am pregnant with twins," I said.

"Really? That's good!" She said.

I was excited. I showed Mom the list that the doctor gave me to start eating and taking vitamins. I was pregnant, not just pregnant, but with twins. I sat with mom until it was time for her to get off work. We went to the store to pick up the items that the doctor wanted me to get. We made it home, and I told my family and BFF who stayed some distance away. I told her the news of me being pregnant. She was excited about me being pregnant, but she was even more excited to know I had twins.

"Let me guess…by Andrew?" She asked.

"Yeah, by Andrew," I said. I told my sister and dad. They were so excited. In the back of my mind, I was thinking.

How am I going to tell Andrew about me being pregnant and with twins? I called my specialist doctor's office that was still overseeing my injury. I wanted to ask the nurse to ask the doctor if me being pregnant, would create any problems or interference when they remove the tube from my stomach. The nurse told me that she would find out and call me back. The nurse called back shortly sharing that it should not be a problem. I was still thinking about how I was going to break the news to Andrew. I did not want to waste any more time.

Later that day, I called Andrew. I knew if I waited to late at night, he would not pick up the phone then I would have to wait until the next day. Then, I would have to muster myself up again to tell him the news. With talking with my mom and my BFF, I was ready to tell Andrew the news. I called him.

"Hello," he said.

"Hey, what are you doing?" I asked.

"Trying to do a little work," he said.

"Andrew, I cannot hear you. Can you step outside? Your background is too loud," I said.

"Yeah," he said. "What's up?"

"Well, I took a pregnant test at home, and it show double lines," I said.

"Okay," he said.

"I did not want to tell you until I went to the doctor to find out for sure. My mom and I found an OBGYN, and I set the doctor's appointment, and I went. The doctor confirmed I am pregnant," I said. He was quiet on the phone. "Hello," I said.

"Yeah, I'm here," he said.

"Well, I'm pregnant with twins," I said.

"Twins!" He said. I could hear the shock in his voice like when the doctor told me.

"Yeah twins, Andrew. Are you okay?" I asked. "I'm excited, Andrew. Are you excited?"

"No not really," he said.

"Why not Andrew?" I asked.

"Let me call you back," he said.

"Okay," I said. He was not ready to hear that at all.

Later that night, he did not call me back. I did not bother calling him back. I felt like it was best to give him some space to allow that to set in.

CHAPTER 24

Wrong Response

The next morning, Andrew called me.

"Hey, where are you?" He asked.

"I'm at home. Are you coming over here?" I asked.

"Yeah," he said. "We really need to talk about this instead over the phone."

An hour later, he arrived at the house.

"You're pregnant with twins?" He asked.

"Yeah, I'm pregnant with twins, Andrew," I said. "You can go with me to the doctor, I have a follow up appointment that is coming up. I don't understand, Andrew, you seem like you are upset."

"Yeah, I am. I don't need any more kids. You're not pregnant by me," he said.

"Wait, what? Andrew are you serious?"

"I don't know what you been doing in the last past month," he said.

"Oh, don't start that mess, Andrew," I said. "You were the last person I slept with Andrew. You even said it yourself; did you forget?"

"I want a blood test," he said.

"That's fine, Andrew," I said.

"I gotta go," he said. I followed him downstairs to his baby mother's car that he was still driving which did not matter at the time. He opened the driver's door and sat down with the biggest disbelief in his eyes.

"Andrew, I really cannot believe you are doing this to me," I said. He picked up his cigarillo out the ashtray and lit it. "Andrew why are you doing this right now?" He inhaled the cigarillo and blew the smoke in my face. It felt as if he had emptied everything he had in his lungs in my face. "Are you serious? You are going to blow smoke in my face knowing I am pregnant? I asked.

He continued to give me this dead look. He took another puff of the cigarillo. I leaned back. I did not want him blowing smoke in my face again. He snatched the driver's door from me, slammed the door, started the car, and left me standing in the parking lot. I went back upstairs crying out aloud why, why, why? I was wondering why he was so upset with me. I did not understand. All the talks he and I had about having kids of our own, a home, and so much more we had discussed. We were up one minute then down the next, but this one threw me off completely. It felt like a roller coaster ride. I was holding on, but my hands were losing their grip. He was telling me he wanted to get married to me and have a family and build all these different things together as husband and wife. What about all the times he told me he loved me? A part of me was a little taken back by his obnoxious behavior, and the other part of me was not. This rollercoaster relationship was making me confused, dizzy, and silly by the day. I could not understand why I kept getting back in the line of this toxic relationship.

The next day, he texted my phone. I could not believe he was texting me; the way he carried on with me when I told him I was pregnant.

"What are you doing?" He asked.

"Wondering why you are so mad at the fact that I am pregnant," I said.

"I need you to come here," he said.

"Why?" I asked.

"I need you," he texted.

"Call me," I texted back.

He called me.

"Hello," I said.

"What's up?" he said.

"You know what's up Andrew? You were looking at me like you wanted to kill me yesterday Andrew when I told you I was pregnant," I said.

"What are you talking about?" He asked.

"Stop playing Andrew," I said. "You are not happy I am pregnant. Am I alright?

"Come down here and give me some," he said.

"I can't come there. Mom has her car today. Can you take me to my doctor's appointment this week?" I asked.

"Yeah," he said.

"I am not playing Andrew. I really need to go to my doctor's appointment," I said.

"Yeah, I'll take you," he said. "What time is the doctor's appointment?" I told him, and we got off the phone.

Time came for me to go to my doctor's appointment. Andrew texted my phone.

"Are you ready?"

"No, I am not ready yet," I texted back. I heard a knock on the door. I looked out of the window and saw Andrew's baby mom's car, and I knew it was him. I opened the door. I already knew what time it was.

Afterwards, I took a shower and got myself together, and we headed out the door to my liver specialist doctor's appointment.

This appointment was for them to see when they were going to remove the tube. Before we made it to the doctor's office, Andrew began to ask me questions.

"Did you tell this doctor, you were pregnant?" He asked.

"I am today," I said.

"Don't you think that's going to be a problem?" He asked.

"Problem with what Andrew?" I asked.

"You cannot have a baby right now with all that you have going on with your body. You have a tube coming out of your stomach, Caroline," he said.

"Andrew, I called the office the other day and asked them about it," I said. "They said it shouldn't be a problem but to mention it to the doctor on my appointment to make sure."

"Man, you are going to kill yourself trying to have these babies," he said.

"Don't say that, why would you say that, Andrew?" I asked.

"Your body cannot handle that?"

"You don't know what my body can handle," I said.

"Neither do you," he said.

CHAPTER 25

Wearing Shame Like Makeup

We made it to my liver specialist doctor's office. We pulled under the parking deck of the hospital. I was feeling a little hurt about the conversation that we just had in the car. I did not want to have a disturbed look on my face walking into the doctor's office. I tried to shake it off before anyone would notice. Some can hide it better than others. I walked to the desk and signed in. I sat down in the chair beside him. We started talking. I asked him if he was going to come to the back with me. Or was he going to stay out in front until I come back out. He agreed to come with me. They called my name; we walked to the room. We sat there until the doctor came to the room. I was happy to see the doctor that help saved my life. He always had a special place in my heart along with Nurse Mary. We were like family to each other, the staff and me. Nurse Mary came in first and greeted me, and I gave her a hug like always. She asked me was I expecting, I told her yes.

"Yes, I remember you calling and asking about if it would be a problem," she said. I looked over at Andrew. "Doctor Mercedes and I will be right back in here in a few minutes."

Andrew picked up a magazine and started reading. Doctor Mercedes and Nurse Mary came in the room short after. He spoke to Andrew and shook his hand. I gave him a hug. I told him what I had been up to after my injury, and how I had been feeling. I also expressed to him the concerned I had about me being pregnant. He told me the same thing Nurse Mary told me on the phone. He told me when I need to come back to schedule my appointment to have the tube removed. That was music to my ears. We left the hospital.

"You hungry?" He asked.

"Yeah," I said. On the way to get something to eat. Andrew grabbed a cigarillo out of the ash tray and lit it.

What My "Yes" Cost Me

"Andrew are you serious?" I asked. "You know I am pregnant with your kids; I can't be around smoke." He gave me that same look he gave me in the parking lot when I first told him I was pregnant. He inhaled and blew smoke all in my face again. This time I was in the car, and I could not escape. I rolled down the window.

"Look, let me say this to you," he said. "I'm not going to be with you because you are pregnant, okay?"

"You don't have to Andrew. Just help me take care of the kids," I said.

"Kids don't keep no man around," he said.

"Andrew I'm not trying to keep you around. What are you talking about? Why are you flipping out like this? One minute you act like you are okay with it, then you flip," I said. "Please just take me home, don't worry about the food."

He looked over at me, as if I said nothing to him. He dropped me back off at home. I was happy to be back home. I sat on the couch and wonder what was going on around me. I started cooking because I was hungry, and I knew Mom would be home soon. Once Mom made it home, I told her the news about the tube getting pulled. Mom's main concerns were making sure I was following the OBGYN's orders and eating and taking my vitamins and the pulling of the tube. I told her that Andrew was not taking me being pregnant too well.

"I don't know why he is not taking it too well. You both were doing what it took to get a baby," she said. My mom never held back on speaking what was on her mind.

"Yeah, mom you're right," I said.

"He does not have to like it. He just needs to be a man and help you take care of these babies," she said.

"Yeah, mom that's what I told him," I said.

Mom was so excited she had already picked out names for them. "Stacey and Tracey" were the names she picked out. I called Andrew to see if he wanted to go with me to the OBGYN appointment. Not sure if he was going to pick up the phone or not.

"Hello," he said.

"Hey are you busy?" I asked.

"Yeah, but what's up?" He asked.

"Do you want to go with me to the OBGYN appointment?" I asked. He hesitated for a minute.

"I got to make sure the truck's running on the road," he said.

"Okay," I said. "I'll let you know how the appointment goes."

CHAPTER 26

Blue Heart

I was still a little taken back from the response Andrew had been giving me since I told him that I was expecting. I scheduled a late OBGYN appointment that day because I had to drop off my mom at work. The overwhelming feeling of hurt and rejection was still present. After dropping off my mom, I came back home, got dressed and ready for the appointment. On my way to the OBGYN's office, I wanted to call Andrew, but I did not want to get myself all upset before going to my appointment. I made it to the doctor's office and signed in at the front desk. As I was walking back to sit down, my phone went off. Andrew texted me asking had I made it to the doctor's office yet. I guess he remembered the text I sent him about the OBGYN appointment. I texted back letting him know I had made it, and I would call him and give him the update. I was excited that he reached out to me making sure I made it to the office.

The nurse called my name and directed me to a room and gave me an overview about what the doctor was going to do as she did before. While sitting in the room all by myself during this process, I felt that it was very selfish of Andrew to have me going through this by myself. Then again, it might not have been a bad idea based off the fact that he was still upset with me. The nurse came in the room and asked me to come out and step on the scale.

"Well, you lost a pound since the first visit." I thought I was gaining weight. I knew I was eating and drinking a lot of milk and food. The doctor walked in and greeted with a handshake. He said he wanted to go over a couple of things with me first before doing the ultrasound.

"Well, I see you lost some weight," he said. "Are you drinking the milk like I ordered you to do?" He asked.

"Yes, I am," I stated.

"Well, I'm not too sure about that. Your weight is saying otherwise," he said.

"I am drinking milk every day," I said.

"How much milk are you drinking?" He asked. "I'm going to need you to drink more and eat more than what you are doing. You have to eat for 3 now," he said.

"Yes, sir," I responded. He directed me to lay back on the exam table so he could do the ultrasound.

As the doctor was doing the ultrasound, he said, "Well, one of the heartbeats is very high and the other one has a normal heartbeat."

I asked him was that okay.

"Yes! Maybe one is going to be more active than the other," he said. "Between you and the dad, which one is the laid back one, and which one is extremely active?" he asked, laughing. "But everything was good. We just have to get you eating more, Mom."

I left out the room and went to the front desk and scheduled the next doctor's visit. I left the doctor's office feeling happy. I called my mom to tell her what the doctor said, "He told me I needed to start eating a lot more for three." She was happy to hear that. I told her I was headed that way to pick her up from work. After picking Mom up from work, I asked her if I could go to Tallahassee. "Yes, Carolina," she said. We stopped to get something to eat before taking mom home. I took my food with me.

Before pulling off, heading to his house, I tried calling Andrew to let him know, I was coming. He picked up the phone. I told him I wanted to show him the ultrasound. "Okay," he said. I was happy to show him the ultrasound. I made it to Tallahassee, grabbed my food from the car. I knocked on the screen door and Andrew came to open the door for me. We spoke to each other, and I walked in and sat down on the chair. Andrew had a sick look on his face.

"Are you okay Andrew?" I asked.

"I've been vomiting all morning long," he said.

"Guess I'm the one doing the eating and you are the one doing the vomiting," I said.

He just crawled up in a fetus position on the sofa, he did not say anything back. He did not find that too funny. I opened my food and started to eat. After I finished eating, I tried to make small talk with him.

"Hey, I got something for you to see," I said.

"What's that?" He asked. I pulled out the ultrasound picture and gave it to him. He sat up on the sofa and looked at it for a minute. He did not show any emotions at all at first. He looked at me smiled and asked.

"Are you happy now?" He asked.

"Why? Are you not happy?" I asked. "Why has your heart grown cold towards me."

"I did not want any kids right now," he said.

"You and I talked about it," I said. He handed the picture back to me. I put it in my pocket. "What are we going to name the kids?"

"You name them," he said. "You set me up, you are out to get me."

"What are you talking about Andrew?" I asked. "You sound crazy. Are you serious? I can't believe you would say that to me. Andrew, I did not get myself pregnant, it took both of us." I got up and went to the kitchen and threw away my trash. "I'm leaving. I just came down here to show you the ultrasound, hoping that you had a change of heart," I said, "but I see you have not changed." He did not say anything. I walked out and got in the car and headed back home.

I cried all the way home. I wanted to get all my crying out before I made it back home. It was like he had a blue heart. A heart with no blood flowing through it, no blood going in or out. A heart with no oxygen. The question I asked myself. Why has his heart hardened towards me? Why is my heart still pumping love for him? I do not understand it. Does he not remember anything he told me? Before I had the injury and afterwards? How could my getting pregnant cause your heart to turn blue? The bigger question was, why was I still hanging around trying give life to something that had already turn blue?

God is the only person who can change the heart of a person, not us.

I made it home and looked in the rearview mirror. My eyes were red from all the crying that I just finished doing. I had to get passed mom without her taking notice of my eyes. I walked straight to my room and to the restroom.

"Carolina," my mom yelled out.

"I'm in the restroom mom," I stated.

"Okay," she said.

I eventually came out of the restroom. I laid on the bed, and I turned my face towards the wall. Minutes later, my mom came in the room.

"I didn't know you was out the restroom. She said. "I have my appointment coming up for the tube to be removed". I stated.

"Okay, I'll try to see if they will let me take off work," she said.

CHAPTER 27

What's Drawing Me Back

It is nothing like waking up to the smell of bacon cooking in the kitchen by my mom. I got up and went to the kitchen to tell her good morning. I went in the restroom and got myself together. Today would have been the day the tube got removed. However, the hospital decided to push back the surgery. I could not understand why I still wanted to keep any communication with Andrew. I picked up the phone and called Andrew.

"Hello," I said.

"Hey," He responded.

"Well, I was just calling you to let you know they pushed the date back for the tube getting removed," I said.

"Okay," he said. He did not sound like he was feeling too well.

"Well, I'm not going to hold you up," I stated.

"What are you fixing to get into?" He asked.

"I'm getting ready to go and eat breakfast."

"Okay," he said. "Come down later on."

"Why what's going Andrew?" I asked.

"Nothing going on," he said.

"Okay," I said. We hung up the phone.

I went in the kitchen and ate breakfast with my mom. I asked her could I use the car. I called Andrew to see if he was at home. He picked up the phone and asked me to come there and he would be waiting on me. One minute he is up, and the next minute, he is talking down to me. I was feeling nervous as I pulled up in the yard. I saw Andrew walking back and forth around on the porch in his white tee shirt. I got out the car, and he opened screen door for me. We walked inside the house. I sat down on the sofa. "What are we doing Andrew?"

"What are you talking about?" He asked.

"We are not going to play these games today Andrew," I stated. "Are we going to be together or what?"

"Yeah, we are going to be together," he said.

"Are you saying that because I'm expecting?" I asked.

"That's why I called you here," he said.

"Andrew, you say one thing like we are going to get married and have kids, then you say it's over."

"I'm going to marry you Carolina", he said. "We going to get married."

"Stop playing Andrew," I said. "When Andrew?"

"I want us to get married in Hawaii," he said.

"When Andrew?" I asked.

"Soon," he said. I was excited. He became this loveable guy all over again.

The part I did not understand about me was why and what was driving me back into his arms and this dysfunctional relationship? The problem became me not him. What was the driving force behind all of it? I never ever been anything this crazy before, what is going on with me?

"Andrew, I don't want you to feel like you got to marry me because I am pregnant," I said.

"I know that" he said.

I headed back home happy about us getting married. While driving back home, Andrew and I stayed on the phone just until I made it back home. I was expressing how I wanted the kids to have the best education there was by enrolling them into Montessori Academy and so much more.

"Wait, wait let's not move to fast," he said.

"What are you talking about let's not move to fast?"

"Well, I think right now is not a good time to have kids," he said.

"I'm pregnant Andrew. "

"I think you need to get abortion," he said.

"Whatttt?" I asked.

"Think about it babe, we need to get married first, then have kids/babies later on," he said. "We need to get this business up and running."

"No Andrew," I said.

"Just think about baby," he said. "No, you need to get an abortion." We argued back and forth on the phone for about hour. "Baby, I wanted to marry you before you told me you was pregnant. I just did not let you know when I was going to marry you." I don't understand Andrew," I stated.

"Andrew abortion why?" I asked.

Weeks later, he called me and asked me was I ready to get married. This was what I had been waiting for. The time had finally come. We were going to have the wedding in Hawaii. He picked me up, and we drove downtown to the courthouse. Before he and I made it to the courthouse. He called someone on his cellphone. I asked him who was he talking to on the phone.

"I had to call somebody," he said.

"Who?" I asked.

He said a guy friend of his. Andrew was talking in code on the phone. Andrew picked up a receipt that was laying in the cupholder and pen and wrote on the back of the receipt. He put the receipt in his jacket pocket. I was not sure what the guy was saying on the other end of the phone. Andrew was saying things like give me the address to the guy on the phone he was talking with. "Yeah, she with me," before hanging up the phone. We made it to the courthouse. We both got out the car. Before walking into the courthouse, we had to go through the metal detector. Once we cleared the detector. We walked down this long hallway. He was so quiet, but I was so happy. I felt that was a little strange. We made it to the counter to fill out the forms for the marriage license. We filled out the paperwork. The lady at the desk that was assisting us with the license told us we had a certain time to bring back the license. I told her, "Okay!" with so much excitement in my voice. On the way out while walking to the car, I asked him, "What pastor are we going to use to marry us?"

"I got us one," he said. With a smile on his face, "You're finally Mrs. Mills," he said. Reaching over giving me a kiss. I kissed him back with no smile on my face and said, "Yes!"

CHAPTER 28

My "Yes" Cost Me

In February 2011, I was excited to be getting married to Andrew.

"Yes, I'm ready to become Mrs. Mills," I said inwardly. I felt some uncertainty about what was getting ready to happen because of that recent phone call. Andrew, finally decide to make me his other half. Through the fights, argument we had made up. I was the one he had chosen. We had already discussed the living arrangements. I was going to move down to Tallahassee. We drove off from the courthouse. "Where are we going Andrew?" I asked.

"You will see when we get there," he said. Andrew pulled out the receipt that was in his front pocket. He then put the address in the GPS on his phone. We pulled up to this building.

"Where are we, Andrew?" I asked.

"You ready?" he asked.

"What are you talking about?" I asked.

"You know we talked about this already," he said. "We are not ready for a baby right now."

"Why Andrew, why?" I asked.

"Baby come on and do this, so we can get married. We can have kids once we get settled," he said. We get out the car and walked in the building. I was feeling horrible, hurt, confused, not understanding why the man I love wanted me to do this. As we were standing at the window, I signed my name on the paper. Andrew put his arm around my waist. He pulled out this large lump of money out of his pocket and handed it over to the lady behind the desk. We went and sat down in the lobby.

"It's okay baby," he said.

In my mind I was thinking, why am I doing this? I thought about just walking out. He sat there with me until they called my name. He kissed me on the forehead and said, "I'll be right back I got to make a phone call."

I looked back at him with hurt and pain in my heart. How did I get to this place? My mind was racing. Should I do this, or should I not do this? The lady called my name to come to the back. Hours later, I come from the back. The lady assisted me back to the front lobby into a chair. As I am sitting in the lobby, I am looking around. I did not see Andrew anywhere. I called him, and he answered the phone.

"Where are you, Andrew?" I asked.

"I'm heading back there," he said.

As I was sitting, waiting on Andrew to come back and pick me up from the clinic. These emotions of hurt and pain came over me again, just worse this time. Thoughts just replaying in my mind over and over of what just took place. I prayed for years to have kids, and now I just did this. How could I allow someone to talk me into doing this? I waited over 10 years or more. I did not think I could have kids in my first marriage, but now I have twins. I felt empty, hurt, pain, confused even the more. I blamed myself over and over. I took full responsibility for it now and then. I felt like I let God down, my kids, myself, my mom, my dad, my sister, and everyone else that was looking forward to embracing the life of my twins. I looked up and there was Andrew walking through the door.

"Babe, are you okay?" He asked. I started crying on my way out the door. I did not answer him. He helped me to the car. "I'm going to drop you back off at the apartment."

"No, you are not," I said. I was afraid to tell my mom. I knew she was going to be so hurt.

"I got to handle some business," he said.

"Nooooo," I yelled with tears running down my face. He drove me to my mom house anyway. We pulled into the parking lot.

"I need you to get out," he said.

"Nooooo, I'm not getting out. You are going to sit in this mess with me. You played a major part in this too," I said. He got out of the car and walked over to the passenger side door and open the door.

"Come on," he said.

"I am not getting out of the car," I said. I sat there for a second.

"Okay. I'll take you to a hotel," he said. I jumped out the front seat and got in the back seat of the car. We drove off. As he was driving.

"Why did you do this to me?" I asked. I started hitting the back of the driver seat. Screaming and yelling, "Why! Why! You killed my babies! You killed my babies."

"Stop, stop! He said.

We made it to the hotel. He went inside the hotel. I sat in the back seat, uncontrollably crying. He came out of the hotel. We drove around the back. He came to the back of the car and opened the door.

"I'm going to stay here with you," he said. "I know you are hurt." We walked to the room. I walked in the room and sat down. I went to the restroom, and I heard the hotel room close. I flushed the toilet and washed my hands. I came out the bathroom, and he was gone. I screamed at the top of my lungs. I sat on the floor and began to cry over and over and over. My phone rang, and it was my mom calling. I could not pick up the phone just yet. I was stuck in the hotel with nothing, no food, no car, no nothing. Later that night, I eventually called my mom to let her know I was okay. I was trying to change the tone in my voice, so she would not notice anything wrong. That did not work.

"What's wrong with you? Why do you sound like you've been crying or stuffy?" she asked.

"I'm okay, Mom," I said. She was not buying that lie. I rushed to get off the phone before any more questions came. THIS IS WHAT MY YES COST ME!

CHAPTER 29

Aborted the Promises

As I was laying in the bed at the hotel. I began to cry out again. I was not ready to tell anyone what just happened. I called my colleague that I went to school with to tell her what happened. I knew I could not call my mom or any of my family and tell them what just happen yet because I was to shameful, guilty, hurt, of "What my "Yes" cost me." I had just "shed innocent blood." According to Apostle Kimberly Daniels, *"The Demon Dictionary. Vol.1,* I had just allowed the spirit of Molech, and Lilith enter into my womb. They are the spirits who avowed enemy of newborn babies. I had owned my part I played in it. I never disown my part. Never abort the gift and blessing that God gives you. It is distasteful in mouth of the Lord, and it is abomination. According to WHO (World Health

Organization), about 40-50 million abortions are performed worldwide each year. Which is about 125,000 abortions every single day. Abortion is the leading cause of death in the world. Second is heart disease, then cancer. Fight for your baby. Your child has an enemy that does not want them to make it out the womb, and he/she is depending on you to fight for them.

I lost my mind. If you are thinking about having an abortion right now, STOP and think about it. I am telling you from experience. The weight of that abortion. It cost me daily. It cost me my state of mind, unsettled rest at night and during the day, it cost me my peace. God will not ever tell you to kill, steal and destroy.

According to John 10:10 (msg), *"the devil comes to steal and kill and destroy,"* God says, *"I came so they can have real and eternal life, more and better life than they ever dreamed of."* You've got to recognize what voice you are going to listen to. If someone says they "love you" and asks you to have an abortion, they do not love you nor themselves. It not only affects you but also the person who tells you to have the abortion. Whatever the enemy is trying to get you to rationalize as to why you should have an abortion, DON'T DO IT. You are carrying God's greatest gift in your womb.

Never compromise with the enemy. I went to the bathroom and sat on the floor and began to cry uncontrollably. I did not care how dirty the floor was in the bathroom. I felt dirtier on the inside than the bathroom floor. How could somebody, like myself, claim that I love the Lord and turnaround and do this to Him? I felt horrible. All the prayers I prayed about having children. Then, to go and do something that is abomination in God's eyesight.

I went back and laid on the bed. I was in a dark, dirty place. I just knew it was no coming back from this dark place. Before this happened, I walked around like I was this wholesome person, and to turnaround and do this. In my mind, how can God forgive me? My mind was messed up. I did not feel even worthy to pray. How can God use a person like me? I just allowed the enemy to hijack my mind. It did not stop there. When the devil got started, he felt like he needed to finish it.

I picked up my phone and called Andrew. Still, no answer from him. I sent him several text messages all night long. I was not going to sleep until I heard back from him. All night long with no sleep. I texted and called Andrew all night long. Seven o'clock that morning I got an answer from Andrew. I was screaming through the phone.

"COME GET ME NOW!" I spoke.

"I will be there in a couple of minutes", he said.

"Look I had to go and take care of some business," he stated. Andrew made it to the hotel. He knocked on the hotel door. "I'm sorry," he said. I was not buying it all. We got in the car.

"Why Andrew? Why Andrew? I asked.

"What are you talking about?" He asked. "Where do you want me to take you?"

I felt like trash. I felt like he needed to drop me off to the nearest dumpster. I was now his trash that he no longer needed or wanted anymore. No matter how I tried to make everything right for him. It was never good enough for him. Do not ever allow anyone to mishandle you or make you feel like you are trash or treat you like you are nobody because in the Lord's eyes you are beautiful and precious. Never depend on a person's validation.

"Take me to my aunt's house," I said.

"Babe, I think you need to go and get some help," he said. I reached over and started hitting him while he was driving. "Stop, stop, stop crazy a** woman," he said. I began to put a plan into action.

"Take me to my aunt's house," I stated. We made it to my aunt's house. I got out of the car and walked slowly to the front door and knocked. My cousin answered the door, and I walked in the house. And what I truly needed at that moment was a hug that I felt I didn't deserve.

"Hey Carolina," he spoke. I could hardly speak back to him. My aunt came out of the back room.

"What's wrong with you?"

I started crying, "Aunt Peaches," that's what we called her. "I had an abortion," I said.

"What?" she said. "Why did you do that Carolina?"

Crying, "I just can't tell my mom."

"Who took you? Andrew?" She asked.

"Yes," I said. I told her everything from the marriage situation to the clinic.

"So, he tricked you into having an abortion," she said. "He is low down."

"I'm going to hurt him. He hurt us. He hurt us. I'm going to hurt him. I got to kill him," I said.

"No, you can't do that," she said. "If you do that you going to prison. Get yourself together."

What My "Yes" Cost Me

I went to the bathroom to dry my face. I came out of the bathroom. "Aunt Peaches, can I use your car?, I asked.

"Where you trying to go?" She asked. "You can use it, but don't go where he is," she said. I started back crying. I sat down in the living room on the couch. I looked through my phone to see who I could call to take me to Tallahassee. I ran across my neighborhood "Big Sister." I called her. She answered up the phone.

"Hello," she said. "Hey Big Sis! Are you busy?" I asked.

"Naw, what's up?" She asked.

"Do you mind dropping me off in Tallahassee?" I asked.

"Where Andrew stays?" She asked.

"Yeah", I said.

"Okay. Once my truck is back from the store. Ronald ran to the store. He will be back shortly," she said.

"Where you at?" She asked.

"Over my Aunt Peaches house," I stated.

"Okay, I'll call you when I am heading that way," she said.

"Okay." I went back into my aunt's house and sat on the couch.

"Carolina, what are you thinking about?" She asked.

"Nothing", I said. I could not tell her I had a ride on the way to pick me up to take me to Tallahassee.

"Carolina, leave it alone; let God take care of him." she said.

"Okay", I said.

After 30 minutes passed. I began to get impatience. I was going to give "Big Sister" some time to pick me up. I was waiting anxiously looking at my phone waiting on her to call me. Twenty more minutes had passed, then my phone rang.

"Hello," I said.

"I'm on my way," she said.

"Okay." I replied.

Minutes later, Big Sis called me back.

"Hey, I'm outside."

"Here I come." My Aunt Peaches looked at me.

"Don't go do anything crazy, Carolina," she said.

"I'm not," I stated. I told a lie to my aunt.

CHAPTER 30

Carrying Out the Mission

I walked outside and got in the truck.

"Hey girl, thanks for taking me to Tallahassee," I stated

"No problem, little sis,"

Big Sis was one of those type of friends/sisters that is ready to ride with you on whatever the agenda might be, good or bad. She had your back, but what I had in mind, I could not tell her my real agenda. I wanted to leave her out of this. We headed down the highway.

"Girl, you still fooling with crazy Andrew?" She asked.

"Yeah", I replied.

"They say that boy ain't no good," She stated.

"Yeah," I said. I switched the subject.

"What are you doing today, girl?" I asked.

"My niece has a birthday party today".

"Oh okay," I said. The conversation ended back to Andrew.

"Is he going to bring you back?" She asked.

"Yeah"

He had no clue I was heading there, but I did not let her know that. We made to Tallahassee. I told her what street to turn on because I did not want anyone to notice me in her truck. She had no tint on the windows. I knew Andrew's little homies that stood on the corner. She pulled up to his house, no vehicle was in the yard. I was looking around to see if I saw his watch dogs sitting on the corner. I did not see anyone on the corner.

"Girl, he's not here," she said.

"It's okay Big Sis," I replied.

"Are you sure?" She asked. "I can sit with you until he comes home."

"Naw, I'm okay, Big Sis. You have a birthday party to go to," I replied. I got out of the truck. "Thanks, Big Sis."

"I don't feel right leaving you here, girl," she stated.

"No, I'm okay," I responded. I did not want "Big Sis" involved in what was getting ready to take place.

She slowly drove off. I went to the porch and knocked on the door. I tried to open it, and it was locked. I remembered what Andrew taught me years back. I went to the side window and pushed it up and stepped one foot on the step. Then I reached my arm inside the window and unlocked the screen porch door. I jumped down and opened the front screen porch door. I walked inside the screen porch. I checked to see if the front door was unlocked, but it was locked. I started just walking around inside the screen porch thinking. I looked over at a shot gun that was on this rack. There were 3 large, black trash bags sitting on the side trying to cover the guns up. I looked inside of the large trash bags, and it was a lot of clothes in all three. As I was moving the bags and clothes around, I saw the bullets that matched the shot gun. It is crazy how the devil can try to assist you with carrying out the mission. This was the perfect setup. I have the gun and the bullets. It had to be meant for me to carry out this insane plan. Immediately, my correctional training kicked in and I made sure the shot gun was loaded and ready. I heard a car coming outside. I jumped behind all those clothes and sat there for a second. I did not hear a car door slam. So, I slowly got up off the floor and looked out the window. I began to take some of the clothes out of the bag so I could cover myself up. I even began to put clothes over the gun as I was laying down on the floor.

Hours went by, and I was still sitting and hiding underneath all those clothes. My legs began to get numb. When he come through the front screen door, I was going to wait until he made it inside good before I carried out the plan. Some more hours had passed. I heard a car pull up. I got the gun ready. I heard the window open for him to unlock the front screen door.

He stepped inside the porch as he was reaching into his pocket to get the key. I moved to point the gun at him. He stopped and looked down over at the clothes and ran over there. I tried to shoot him. He and I started to wrestle over the gun. I did not want to shoot myself with the gun. He stands 6'2", and I stand 5'6". As we were still tussling over the gun, I am trying to pull the trigger. We continued to tussle back and forth, up and down. Finally, he got the gun out my hand. With tears coming down my face, I yelled out, "Why did you do that to me and my babies?" I asked with heavy breathing. I charged towards him. He picked me up and carried me inside the house. We were standing in the living. He walked over to the corner of the living room by the TV.

"Answer me! Why did you do that?" I continued to ask.

"I'm the devil's son," he stated. He called out a name that I could not hear well and gave me this look like something off a scary movie.

"SAY WHAT?" I asked. "What did you just say to me?"

He did not repeat himself at all. He walked over to the kitchen. I walked over to the kitchen behind him. Repeat what you said, I asked.

"What do you mean you are the devil son? What the hell?" I replied backed. I started hitting him. He picked me up and carried me outside the house.

"Come on. I'm taking you home," he said.

"No, you are not," I responded. He tried to force me into the passenger side of the car. As we were tussling again. I snatched away from him kicking him. The neighbors started to come outside. "I'm not getting in the car with the devil's son." The driving demonic force that was behind him that cause him to carry out what he did was the same force I had yielded to want me to take his life.

I wanted to hurt Andrew so bad. I had allowed the devil to sleep with me and steal, kill, and destroy me.

When a person tells you who they really are believe them. I heard it so much growing up, it became cliché to me. I really did not believe it after hearing it so much. But I had to find out the hard way. It's different when it hits home to you. I was sleeping with the devil's son. Are you kidding me? I started walking down the street. I heard the car following behind me.

"Leave me alone," I yelled out. I had not made it to the stop sign at the end of the corner.

CHAPTER 31

Help Me Please, Lord

With Andrew still following behind me in the car. I walked on the right side of the street. I was getting closer to the stop sign. He stopped the car and walked around the car, trying to get me to get in the car.

"Just get in the car. I'll take you home," he said.

"No, I will walk home," I stated. He jumped back in the car. I started back walking, and I made it to the stop sign. I crossed the street to the other side of the highway and started walking in the grass trying to stay out the way of the traffic on the highway. As I continued walking in the grass, tears were filling up in my eyes. I looked down at the ground as I walked because I did not want anyone to see me crying.

As I continued to walk down the highway, I briefly looked up, and I saw a sign I would always see when I would drive on my way home. "Beware of hitchhiking." It was a prison unit right down the street. At that time, I did not care about any of that with the hurt, pain, anger, feeling lost, confused state of mind I was in. All these emotions I was feeling on the inside while I was walking down the highway. I did not care about that sign. I looked up and saw Andrew car passing me going in the direction I was walking. I saw a car traveling on the opposite side of the highway. It slowed down just enough to have a guy hanging out the back side of the window on the driver side. He yelled out.

"Are you okay ma'am?" He asked.

"Yes, I'm okay. Thanks," I replied, and they continued driving. As the cars continued to pass me on the highway, I began to talk with God inwardly, not knowing if he would even hear me or listen after all the dishonorable things I had done in His eyesight. "MA'AM STOP!" I stopped walking and turned around.

"Are you okay ma'am?" He asked.

"Yes, I am," I said.

"I got a call from Andrew. He wanted me to check on you, and plus, there are calls coming in about you," he said.

"Sir, I am okay. This is embarrassing," I said.

"What is embarrassing?" he asked.

"You sir, a Sheriff, stopping me on the side of the highway", I said.

"Did he hit you or anything?" he asked.

"No, he did not," I said.

"Where are you headed? Can I call somebody to come and pick you up?" He asked.

"I am headed to Monroe," I replied.

"That is a long way from here, ma'am", he said.

"I'll be fine", I said.

"Okay are you sure?" he asked again.

"Yes, I am fine thanks!"

"Okay ma'am", he said. He drove off, and I continued walking down the highway

"Lord, please forgive me. Lord I am so sorry. Help me, Lord please!" I cried out to him with a heavy heart. "Please forgive me."

I lifted my head up, and I saw cars after cars passing me on the highway. A particular car stopped in the middle of the highway traveling in the same direction I was walking. No cars were coming behind it. The car went in reverse and backed up to me while I continued to walk. A young lady rolled down her passenger side window.

"Are you okay?" She asked.

"Yeah, I'm okay,". As I was trying to restrain the sniffles.

"I know you say that, but it doesn't appear as if you are ma'am," she replied. I never stopped walking. She kept her window down and drove her car at speed of my walk. "Can I take you somewhere, ma'am?" She asked.

"No, I'm okay I can walk, thanks," I responded.

"Do you mind me asking where are you going to? I don't mind taking you to where you need to go," she said.

"I'm going home with tears flowing down my face." I heard a car coming behind us. The car began to honk the horn at her car. "Ma'am, a car is coming behind you, I'm okay."

"They can go around," she said. She rolled down her driver side window and signal the car behind to go around. "Where do you stay?" She asked.

"I stay in Monroe," I stated.

"That's a long way from here ma'am. I'm going that way," she said. "I don't mind giving you a ride," she said. As I continued to walk, I saw Andrew coming up the highway on the opposite side. I immediately stopped talking. "Ma'am are you okay? What's wrong? Is somebody after you?" She asked.

"No, I'm okay," I said. I thought he was going to keep going. He did a U-turn in the middle of the highway. He drove the car on the opposite side of me with one side of the car in the ditch. I was sandwiched between both cars. The young lady was on my left side, and Andrew was driving on the other side. He rolled down his driver window.

"Just get in the car," he said.

"No leave me alone Andrew,"

"Hey," the young lady yelled out across to him. "Are you bothering her?" The braveness the young lady had was remarkable. Most individuals would have felt like it was not their fight, and they are not going to get in it.

"What?" He asked.

"Are you messing with her?" She repeated.

"No, I'm not bothering her. What are you talking about?" He asked.

"Is he bothering you ma'am?" She asked.

"I'm okay,"

"I'm not going to leave you here with him," she stated. Andrew took off in the car in full speed ahead of us. "I got his license plate," she said.

I could not understand how someone that does not know me could care so much. She was a stranger to me. Then a thought crossed my mind. Only if she knew what just took place. The more I thought about it, I began to break down. I had to stop walking. With both hands down on my knees, I broke down and started crying profusely. I felt like trash all over again.

"Come on, ma'am, get in the car," she stated. "I'm not sure what happened but it's going to be okay. Ma'am you would have to walk 22 miles. That's too far for you to be walking," she responded.

CHAPTER 32

Catching A Ride With An Angel

"Okay," I said.

I took her up on her offer to give me a ride home. My legs were getting weaker from the walking. I felt so disconnected as to who I was as a person, and as a woman. I lost my integrity. All of it was questioned at this point. I felt so ashamed on every level.

"I'm too dirty to be in your car," I said.

"No, you are not," she stated.

I literally meant outside and inside. I wanted to tell her, *ma'am, I had just taken a shotgun moment earlier and just tried to hurt who just hurt me and my kids*. If I would have told her what really happen, would she put me out of her car and tell me to catch another ride? Which I would not blame her if she wanted too. As we were riding down the highway, I thought about what the lady told me at the clinic about taking it easy not to be moving around a lot. Here I was walking down a highway feeling like I was losing my mind and in need of help. The enemy had bombarded my mind again. I felt like a failure, I failed myself and kids again because I did not carry out the plan that was intended. I wanted Andrew to pay for what he did.

"You are okay, ma'am. You are not dirty," she said.

I was not sure if she was just being honest or just trying to be polite when I told her I was too dirty to be in her car. I took it has her being polite. I knew I had not taken a bath.

"My name is Angela," she said. "What is your name?"

"Carolina,".

"I was not going to leave you until you got inside this car," she replied.

"Thank you," I said.

"I was going to ride my car right along the side of you until you got tired of walking," she stated.

In my mind, I was thinking only if she knew what just took place. Would she still be this warm and kind to me?

"I was going to call my mom and sister and let them know I was going to be a late," she said.

"I'm sorry for holding you up," I responded.

"No, it is okay. My twin and my birthday are coming up, and my mom wanted to take us out to eat," she said.

"YOU ARE A TWIN?" I asked. I was in a state of shock. I just broke down and cried again.

"Are you okay?" She asked. I was too ashamed to tell her what just happened to my twins.

I was thinking, "What are the odds of me riding in a car with a twin, young lady." Hebrews 13:2(msg) says, *"Don't forget to be kind to strangers. For some who have done this have entertained angels without realizing it."* In my mind, I knew we were strangers to each other, but never in a million years would I have thought I would be riding in a car with a twin.

I took this as a sign from God. I thought about the prayer I had with God while I was walking. Did God just send a twin angel to come and pick me up? No, not me. I just did the unthinkable, unforgiveable thing in God's eyes. Surely not me. Not only just a ride but a ride from a twin. My mind was messed up even more. After the short ride, we made it to my mother's home. We got out of the car. I began to thank the young lady again for giving me a ride home. I am still in a state of shock to know she is a twin. We walked up the stairs, I put my key in the door. My mom had the lock chain on the door. We had to wait until Mom came to the door to take the chain off. My mom came to the door with a sign of relieve on her face yet worried look.

"Hello ma'am. My name is Angela," the young lady spoke to my mom.

"Hey baby. How are you doing?" Mom asked. I sat down on the couch. "What happened, Carolina?"

"She gave me a ride home, Mom," I said.

"Do you mind telling me what happened, Angela?" Angela looked over at me, and I gave a head nod, "yes." She began to tell my mom what happen. My mom took both of her hands and put her face in both hands. "I have been calling and looking for her all day long." "Ma'am I totally understand." Afterwards, Angela stood up and headed to the door. I gave her a hug, and we exchanged numbers.

"I'm sorry, momma," I said. I walked to the back room and closed the door. I wanted to call my dad and tell him what happened to me, but the guilt and shame that I had would not allow me to do it right then. I love my dad so much, but a part of me did not want to tell him. I was afraid of what my dad would say. Mom walked in the bedroom standing in the doorway. I knew this would be the time to tell my mom what had happened to the grandchildren that she longed to have and hold in her arms. I did not want to crush my mom's heart, but I had to tell her the unthinkable thing I had done.

CHAPTER 33

Broken Heart's

"Mom, I had an abortion,"

"No Carolina, why?" She asked with tears rolling down her face. I had just shattered a dream that my mom wanted. Both mine and my mom's heart ripped apart. Even in my mom's pain and hurt, she was still thinking about me. "Do I need to get you some help? Do you need some counseling?"

"Yes, mom please," I stated.

"Call your dad and tell him, "She said.

Another broken heart I had to crush with this distasteful action that I have done. The last thing I wanted to do was break my mom and dad or sister's hearts. I always wanted my dad and mom to be proud of me since I was a little girl. It was never my intention to break their hearts. I did not want to tell my older sister because I knew she would be hurt also. She was looking forward to being an auntie. Just another broken heart added on the list to break. I picked up the phone and called my BFF and told her what happened. I could hear the hurt in her voice. Before I could get anything else out, she asked if she needed to come down and see about me. Minutes later, she called back and told me she was on her way to see me; she had gotten the okay from her husband to come and sit with me in my misery. She stayed 2 hours away from me. My BFF and husband had already come to see me at the hospital when I almost died. Now this! I was causing more hurt and pain upon the hearts of those whom I loved and who loved me the most.

I got up and took a shower. As I was standing in the shower, I began to break down. I began to repent over and over. I begged God again for his forgiveness over and over. I asked God. "What do I need to do?" I heard, "Let Go."

Fast forward to months later, every day I had to live with that pain, hurt, shame living in my heart. The thing about having an abortion, it robs you of your joy, your peace, and your true happiness. The stain remover is "Jesus" and His blood that washes you clean. I eventually told my dad, but the response that he gave me was so loving. He did not condemn me. He loved me despite the most miserable thing I had done. My mom did the same thing. I did enough of condemning and hating myself every day that I woke up to each morning. I could not find it in myself to forgive me. I did not feel the worthiness of being forgiving for the sins I had committed.

Whatever you feel like you could not be forgiven for. Just "REPENT" ask the Lord to forgive you for it. Just think about what Jesus has already done on the cross for you and me. That does not give you a right to live the way to want to live, but love God enough to not hurt Him. It is only through Jesus's death and resurrection what restored our broken relationship with

God. Let the truth be told we all are not worthy but because "Jesus" died on the cross for us that makes us worthy in God's eyes. Just as my earthly Father loved me despite the horrible sin I had committed. My Heavenly Father loves me much more.

Our Heavenly Father who knew us even before we were in our mother's womb. He loved me and had already forgiven me. "Agape Love." Sometimes I could not wrap that around my mind. Something was blocking me from accepting that in my heart and mind. Months later, I still had a battle going on in my mind. I had a couple of text messages from Andrew every now and then. I could not believe that I was still entertaining him. The devil's son is what he called himself. What was wrong with me? The text messages that Andrew was sending were how sorry he was for the part he played in getting that abortion. I had to take my part of ownership in it. I never should have listened to the lies. I tried to move pass it, but I was stuck. I was still trying to stop thinking about what had taken place in my life, but nothing seemed to work.

One day I was thinking about going down to Tallahassee again to try to get revenge. This time I was taking a knife with me. My pastor, Dr. Pearl, whose leadership I was under reached out to me, and I was just crying out to her about what I was getting ready to do to Andrew. Her and co-pastor came to pick me up from the apartment. She prayed for me, and they took me out to eat. I told her that Andrew said that he was the devil's son. Immediately she said, "Believe him. Cut him loose, Sis. Carolina." The authority in which she spoke, I knew it was true. Because my mind went back to the shower of me hearing "let go." I wanted to share with her about the abortion, but I was still ashamed. But that was not enough. It was a stronghold that I was not built for in the flesh. I needed some major deliverance.

I believe the Lord decides on how He will go about getting the deliverance to a person. You got to want the deliverance. I remember that night I had a dream. In the dream, I saw Andrew standing in his front living room with a white shirt on, but it was strange because suddenly the dream switched over to me getting taken away in a vehicle. I was sitting in the back sit of the vehicle. I looked up at the sky. I saw a huge figure that covered the sky. He had a cone hat on his head. It looked very demonic. The look he gave was as if he was angry with me. He did not scare me at all, but I could not figure out why I was taking away in a vehicle by an unknown person. Then I woke up the next morning and was wondering what that dream was about? I went in the living room and sat down and turned on the Christian television channel and saw that same demonic creature. I said aloud, "God, that is it!" I saw that in my dream. What is that? The man began to describe that figure of being the devil. Is that why he looked at me as if he was mad at me? I was in disbelief because he would visit me in my dream. I got myself together that day and carried on with my day. I tried to shift my focus on something else like the settlement that was coming. Yes, I was getting compensation from the injury that happened to me, but the money could not take away the scars that were embedded in my mind and body, along with the abortion that had just taken place.

What I took away from the dream was I believe it was a sign that I was getting delivered from this relationship. This was something I so desperately needed from my Heavenly Father to do for me along with casting out all strongholds that were keeping me bound to this relationship. Now that I had been sleeping with the devil's son and had continue to sleep with him, I could not break it on my own strength. I needed the relationship to be cut and uprooted. I needed supernatural deliverance to take place now.

CHAPTER 34

Strongholds

Whatever God has told you to let go of, Do it! Andrew and I slowly started back texting each other back and forth, once or twice a month. The relationship just was not the same at all. It was a line that was crossed in the sand. It never felt the same and would never be the same. I would wake up in the morning with the thought of my kids on my mind. The guilt, shame, fear, condemnation, sorrow was part of my everyday garment along with carrying around a travailing womb. I would have never thought that I would have done anything this horrible in my life for anybody. Why? How did I get here? That is why it is so important NOT to link up with just anybody because of their looks, or their charming words. Or involve yourself with sexual ungodly soul ties.

Months came and went. I slowly tried dating other people besides Andrew. That did not work! The strength of the stronghold between Andrew and I had started to weaken slowly day by day. Every day the stronghold was breaking off me. Time was drawing near for me to get the settlement from my injury. Two in half years had passed. Finally, I came into the settlement money. It was money I had never been in contact with before in my life. It was over a quarter of million dollars. Andrew and I's relationship had come to an end. I had moved on to another relationship with another guy for some months now. I had known him since I was in high school. He and I moved to Virginia for a short period of time. I finally got the dream truck I prayed for. I never knew I was going to be able to pay cash for anything this major in my life.

In Genesis 50:20 (msg), *"Don't you see, planned evil against me but God used to those same plans for my good."* I did not know I had to go through all of what I went through to get here to this place. Paying cash for things.

Whatever you are going through right now, just know that it is going to be turned around for your good. Just hold on to God.

I was still thinking and searching out different business ventures. I always had the desire to own a business. I did not really trust too many people. Months had passed. Andrew didn't know anything about me getting my settlement. Andrew and I had texted each other a couple of months after my ex and I had broken it off. Nothing serious at all.

While sitting in my apartment, Andrew and I went from texting to us talking back on the phone. Nothing about getting back together. Andrew was telling me about how he and his drivers were doing good on the road. I was telling him about the different investors I had met up with but not letting him in too much of my business.

"Hey, I'm telling you. I think you should invest in some trailers and let some truck drivers pull them for you. You can lease them out," he said. Our conversation was basically about business. I figured since the relationship part did not work out for us, then maybe the business side could. I did my research on it. He told me where I could purchase some new used grain trailers.

"Hey, let me come down there and show you. I got some kin people there anyway." I never thought that Andrew and I would ever be in each other presence again. He flew down to Virginia. I picked him up from the airport. We drove to one of his relative's home. He pulled out a check book and wrote a check, dropped it off, and we left. His relatives and I went out to eat. I still could not see him the same. After dinner we went back to the apartment. We talked about the trailers and how much I would get back each week from leasing out the trailers. He told me he knew some truck drivers that were looking to lease out trailers. Afterwards, he said he wanted to talk with me about some things. We went and sat in the living room. He began to talk about the twins. He was saying how remorseful he was for doing that to me. He knew talking about my twins was a soft spot in my heart. I saw tears come down his face, something I never saw from him before. All the years I've known him other than when he would talk about his grandpa.

"I'm so sorry for tricking you to do that," he said. "I deal with that every day. I got to make it right with you." It really did not feel right with being with him. Weeks later, I went down to purchase the grain trailers. I looked at the grain trailers and went to the bank and purchased my new grain trailers. It felt good to have at least one business venture going. It felt like I was succeeding in life.

After purchasing the trailers, my other trailers had to be picked up out of town. Andrew agreed that he would go and get them for me. On the way back from Minnesota, he called a couple of his drivers telling them to help me bring these trailers back to Monroe. Once we made it back to Monroe, Andrew told me he knew where the trailers could sit.

"I already got you some drivers lined up baby," he stated.

"Really," I replied.

"You ain't got to do nothing, baby, but just sit back. I'm going to show you a couple of things about the trailers so you will know what you are looking at. You need to know a little something about the trailers, so these guys won't try to get over on you." With so much excitement in my voice. "I'm about to call a couple of drivers up here," he said.

I met some of the drivers, and they began to ask me how much I would be leasing the trailers out for. I told him I will let him know. I had not drawn any leasing agreement papers out just yet. Andrew and the guy walked back up to his truck, and they sat in the truck for little over 30 minutes. I knew I had to move back to Monroe because I wanted to keep an eye on my trailers. My lease on my apartment was coming to an end. I began to look for something close. I was single, not in any relationship. New business, a nurse, money in different banks, yet walking around still a little broken on the inside still but on the path to healing.

People saw the glory but never knew the story behind the glory, or what I had to go through to get what I got and what I continued to go through daily. I found an apartment in Monroe that was between where my trailers were. Andrew was calling me a lot more. He said he was happy I was moving back. He said it is better if we get back together than to be apart. I would own part of his Bar and Grill Lounge. We can pick up where we left off before we broke up. I could not come into agreement with that. That feeling began to come back in my belly how I would feel when I would go to Tallahassee to visit him. He began to show me the building that he was still working on. He and I started back having sex. I ended up getting pregnant twice by Andrew, but I miscarried both pregnancies. I had a traveling womb. The presence of the twins was enlarged in my womb. Even after praying and crying that the Lord healed my womb, I still ended up having a miscarriage. When God tells you to let go of whatever he is trying to deliver you from, do that because going back is much worse.

CHAPTER 35

Cost Of Going Back To What God Said

"Let Go"

Time came for me to move back to Monroe. I noticed that my titles from the trailers had not come in the mail yet. So, I called up to the place where I purchased the trailers.

"Hello, this Carolina," I said.

"Yes, hey I remember you," he replied.

"I'm calling because I have not received my titles from you guys yet, can you tell me why?" I asked.

"Well, you should've gotten them already, Ms. Carolina," he stated.

"I don't have them," I said.

"Andrew called up and told me to put the titles in his name," he responded.

"Whatttt? Nooooo!" I said. I could have dropped the phone.

"Carolina, you have got to be joking me," he said.

"No, I am not," I stated.

"Did he just get over on us?" he said.

"Please tell me you all did not do that," "I did not give you all permission to put anything in his name nor did I give y'all anything in writing.

"Yes, ma'am! We are fully aware those trailers belong to you," he said. "I started to call you ma'am and ask you about it."

"Why didn't you call me and ask?" I stated. I hung up the phone.

I was in shock. I felt dumb because I should've followed up with the trailer company earlier, and why did I get back involved with this thief? Why did I go back to him when God told me to "let go?" I have never looked back. I questioned myself again, why, why, why? But I had to think quickly. I was thinking about all the things he was telling me about how he was sorry for doing what he did to me. How he wanted to get back with me, and how he was still in love with me, and he goes and does something like this! All of that fast talking he was doing, and I fell into his lies again. How could he keep up with all the lies he told? Andrew knew the damage he done in the past to me. I felt so naïve. I should have closed that door for good and left no gap for him to come back into my life.

When you close the door to a relationship make sure you close it for good. Do not entertain the devil or leave an opening for him. According to 2 Corinthians 2:11 (msg), *"We don't want to unwittingly give Satan an opening for yet more mischief-we're not oblivious to his sly ways!"* Which I gave into. I had to think quickly in the middle of receiving the news from the company. I called him, and he picked up the phone.

"What's up Andrew?" I asked. I could barely keep it together while talking to him.

"Nothing," he replied.

"Where are my trailers?" I asked.

"They are over at the place I took you too," he stated. I knew I had to get an attorney quick. I had to make haste moving back to Monroe. My inside was boiling. I could not hold back on asking him.

"I called you Andrew to ask you about those titles. The people at the place said that you have my titles, and I need my titles and trailers," I demanded. He denied of having any titles.

"Don't let those people lie to you about having your titles," he responded.

"Stop playing with me Andrew," I said. "Give me my D*** titles." He hung up the phone in my face.

Weeks later, I had an attorney. She was aware of what we were up against. I told her the beginning of everything to what lead me to hiring her as my attorney.

In between waiting on the case going to court, I would call and plead with Andrew about turning over my titles and trailers that he knew did not belong to him. He began to laugh at me. He began to get bold with me. He told me boldly, "You are not going to get those trailers or titles back." He began to hide the trailers from me and began to hook them up to different trucks. He was trying to sell all the trailers before my attorney, and I could get him in court. I would sit in my truck and cry and ride back and forth to Tallahassee. He had one of my trailers in Tallahassee blocked by sitting an old truck in front of it.

I would call Andrew daily to plead with him to give me back my trailers, the more I called the worse it got for me. I felt like the longer it took for us to go to court the more it felt like I was losing the battle. I would see my trailers riding around town, but I could not do anything at the time. He would call and antagonize with pictures of my trailers and say they were his and that the judge was going to laugh at me. He told me that he was going to lie that we were in a relationship to gain ownership of the trailers, and he would prove to me that he was going to keep those trailers. He had hidden attorneys and sheriffs working for him in his back pocket. I remember praying to God to help me again, but the enemy tried to play with my mind by telling me that the Lord was not going to listen to me. I went ahead and prayed anyway not knowing how the end was going to turn out. I remembered I was led to read 2 Chronicles 20:17, *"You will not have to fight this battle. Take up your positions; stand firm and see the deliverance the Lord will give you, Judah and Jerusalem. Do not be afraid; do not be discouraged. Go out to face them tomorrow, and the LORD will be with you."*

That word took root in my heart. Andrew was telling me that he was going to use every lie against me. It was not looking to promising for me on the outside. He had sheriff's that was telling him not be at the location so he could not be serve the papers. I had to hire a private server to serve him the papers.

CHAPTER 36

Having Victory In A Fixed Fight

It came time for my attorney and I to take Andrew to court. Not sure how the day was going to turn out for me. I got a text message from Andrew telling me how he was going to win. After getting dress and leaving out the door going to court. I sat in my truck and pulled up 2 Chronicles 20:17 on my phone and said it aloud. While driving to the courthouse I began to think about the text messages Andrew had sent me. I made it to the courthouse and scanned the parking lot to see if Andrew had made it before me. I did not see his vehicle but that did not mean anything when it came to Andrew. It was nothing for him to borrow someone else's vehicle to throw me off. I knew all his tricks that he had up his sleeve. I called my attorney to let her know I was at the courthouse. As I walked in the courthouse, I was praying at the same time, hoping I did not run into him before I saw my attorney. Time was getting close for us to go inside the courtroom, and I saw my attorney. She and I went into a room and prayed before going before the judge.

When we came out of the room, my attorney and I saw Andrew and his attorney coming around the corner. Andrew winked at me before he took his seat on the bench. His attorney approached my attorney. Both attorneys stepped aside and went back and forth. She came back and told me that Andrew and his attorney were going to move forward, and that Andrew told his attorney he was not giving me back my trailers or titles. My attorney said, "Let's go and present your case to the judge. How dare he show up with an attorney." He had the nerves to lawyer up on me, knowing that I had purchased those trailers for me and my investment.

It was time for us to enter the courtroom. He and his attorney sat on one side, and we sat on the other side of the courtroom. We had to sit and wait for our names to be called and listen to everyone else's case. As we were waiting to be called to present the case to the judge, my thoughts went back to how he lied to me about everything. Something clicked on inside me. This was a setup from the pits of hell from the beginning. He had it out for me from the beginning of this relationship. The driving force in Andrew came to kill, steal, and destroy everything that was attached to me. He really is the "devil's son."

I cannot believe that this guy would even try to challenge me about something that he knew with no doubt that the trailers nor the titles belonged to him. I was baffled by it. When all he had to do was give me back my trailers and titles. I should have obeyed God when I was told to leave Andrew alone.

Obey God and do not go back. Do what God said. "Let Go." Do not go near it, do not pick it up, do not flirt with it. Going back leaves residue. Do not compromise with the devil. I do not care what it looks like on the outside. If you are reading this book and God has told you to obey him in something, just obey HIM! Ignore the driving force behind the enticement that you are running after. Make sure it is God.

My and Andrew's name were called in the courtroom. I was embarrassed that other people had to sit in the courtroom to listen in on the case, but quickly the nervousness went away. It was time to present my case to the judge. Sure, enough Andrew and his attorney used the lie he said he was going to use against me. His lies and schemes did not work. The Judge awarded my trailers and titles back to the rightful owner which was me. Victory prevailed!

My attorney and I were overjoyed. The judge also told Andrew to pay back what he had sold. I had to give the glory to the Lord and only Him. As I was walking to my truck and heading to get something to eat across the street, my phone went off. Andrew was really upset with my attorney, the judge, and me. He texted he was not going to give me my trailers back no matter what the Judge said. This guy is crazy. This was the judge's orders. I drove across the street to get a burger. Before I could get out the truck, Andrew pulled up on the side of me. With a look of discouragement, I saw him through the window. He was texting me while sitting in vehicle right beside me. "I see you got what you want," he texted.

A month later, Andrew was texting me how he was not going to pay me back and how he was working on the building, and once his building was up and going, he was going to pay me back all my money.

A month later, Andrew told me where I could go and pick up my trailers but still no payment yet from what he had sold as the judge ordered. I had started working on another business venture. I asked my mom if I could move back in with her once my lease was up.

She felt I needed to move far away from Monroe. I could not agree with my mom more. My mom was my right-hand person. When you saw me, you saw my mom. My mom would go to meetings with me. She was my mother growing up, but she became my best friend as I got older. She would still pull her rank as "Mom" when she felt I had forgotten who she was. We would have our disagreements, but through it all we worked through it. We were inseparable.

CHAPTER 37

Love, Celebrate, Wait

I was living back with my mom since my lease was up. I had to find a church home. My mom met a lady that was doing hair. That later became my mom's and my hairstylist. She was telling us about the church she was attending. She invited my mom and me to attend service one Sunday. Everything else was history. I joined the church. I met new fellow church members. I was under a great leadership of a mighty Man/Woman of God that was led by the Spirit of God. I really enjoyed service every time I went. It changed my thought process. Not only that, but the teaching was also helping me outside of the church and in my everyday living.

As time went by, I learned I was a woman in waiting as our great Apostle would say to women that desired to be married. We were "Women in Waiting." I truly was a woman in waiting. But I was not going looking for anything. My past dating experiences let me know I was attracting the wrong guys. I began to seek the Lord truly and love on myself. I began to fall in love with me. I would take trips to Las Vegas by myself and just love on me. I noticed I stop begging God for a husband. The desire was there. I continued to stand on His word and kept my faith. I had accepted that the Lord was my husband until He felt I was ready for an earthly husband. My new business venture kept me busy also. I remember a fellow church member that attended the church. I invited her to come over to this new business venture with me. She came to help me discuss and make different steps to the business.

I remember the day when she came over because it was during "Day of Atonement". Before we got started, we would pray. We were sitting in the kitchen talking, and she began to pray for me. She began to flow in the spirit. She said, "I do not know what this mean, but I am going to say it. I hear the Lord saying, *I could not allow it* to happen again." She took a deep breath afterwards. I began to cry out in the kitchen. I knew what the Lord was saying. My mind went to the miscarriages I had with Andrew and everything else that was tied up with him. The cord had been broken between us. I was able to spend more time with God.

I would go on dates with guys but trust me it was nothing serious. I remember my hairstylist was doing my hair. She had recently gotten married. While she was doing my hair, she told me that she and her husband were doing a couple's party for married couples. I told her my husband and I did not get an invite. She looked at me and said, "Girl you are not married yet." With excitement in my voice, "Umm, yes I am," laughing.

A month had passed, and time came for me to go back to the hair salon to get my hair done. As I was getting my hair washed. I asked her.

"How did the party go?

"Oh, we did not have the party", she said.

I said jokingly, "See you should have invited me and my husband. My husband could have turned y'all water into wine." We both busted out with giggles.

I would pray before I would go to sleep at night. I would say aloud Genesis 2:24 once a night. I must be honest with you. As time came and went, it seemed as if I was surrounded by nothing but married women not on purpose, I think. At times, I did wonder when God was going to release my earthly husband, but I was content.

"There is a purpose behind the waiting period." Don't allow the waiting process to overtake you and allow you to produce a premature "yes" to Ishmael instead on waiting on Issac.

After the Lord cut the cord between Andrew and me, it was a lifetime lesson I had learned and that was to wait on the Lord.

I enjoyed attending other people's weddings and celebrating with them. I remembered when our Apostle's daughter was getting married. I went to the wedding; I was so excited for them. I remember at her wedding at the reception it was time for the bride to toss the bouquet. Traditionally, at most wedding receptions, all the single women will hit the floor and get in position for the tossing of the bride's bouquet. Whomever catches the bouquet is next in line to get married. I did not get in line to catch the bouquet. After the reception was over, I remember telling one of the ladies that I was walking out the door with, I might not have caught the bouquet tonight. But I am going to run in faith believing I'm next in line to get married. And I took off running to my truck and began to praise God.

If you are waiting on that spouse. Remember His timing! He has that right someone for you. Love on the Lord and love yourself. Celebrate with people. While you wait on your special delivery, you are going to know he/she was sent from God. I love the Lord. He has a sense of humor. He knows how to let you know that it is from Him.

CHAPTER 38

God's Love, and Grace, Forgiveness

A year later, I met my husband. God had shown me His grace and mercy once again. God was the orchestrator behind us meeting. My husband, Julius, is from California. Not only is he from a whole other state, but he is an Identical TWIN! Yes, identical twin. What are the odds of that? Julius is a true man of God that loves the Lord just as much as I do. It would be times before he and I got married, we would pray on the phone at 3am.

In February 2016, Apostle Renda married us both in her office. She had already met him prior to us getting married. We went down to that same courthouse that I went to years earlier. In the same month but different year and got married. Julius and my mom hit it off, right away. She loves her some Julius. I am not sure if it is because they shared the same birth month. The "month of love." February has so much significance behind it for me. God not only showed me his love for me and his forgiveness, but my twins, my mom, my husband, and my BFF all share the same birthday month. "Love month." I never saw my mom so happy for me other than my passing the nursing boards. For my mom to find out that he is a twin brought mom and me so much joy. I fell in love with the fact that he would beat me worshipping the Lord. Hallelujah! His outer appearance was the cherry on top. His inner heart lined up with his outer appearance. We got married and moved away to Atherton, CA.

I hope this book inspired many of you. That God is real and His love, grace, and mercy He gives to us is priceless. He shows us daily how much He loves us. We may not understand His ways but that is okay. He did not create us to understand His ways but to trust Him, obey Him, worship Him and have a relationship with Him. It is His love that draws us into a deeper relationship with Him. I also, would like to inspire my readers that my experience would save many from staying too long in the wrong relationship and to keep you from saying the wrong "YES" to something that will COST you.

The moral of sharing my story is to help millions of people globally. No matter the race, ethnicity, and no matter how much money you have. No matter what side of the country you live on. I want you to know that you matter, and the Lord loves you. I want to help people recognize the Ishmael from the Isaac and to help set the captives free from bondage of feeling bound in the wrong relationship with the wrong person. To recognize the RED signs and not to ignore them. Not to override the Holy Spirit when He is giving you instructions. How NOT to compromise with the devil, and to help save millions of babies from being aborted by their mothers.

If you have not been saved and would like to be saved, or not sure about your salvation. IT's Free! Jesus paid it in FULL! Say aloud, "Heavenly Father, I come to you now in Jesus Name. I confess that I am a sinner and that I have sinned against you. I ask you to forgive me for all of my sins and I repent for my sins, and I choose to follow, obey and I accept your son Jesus Christ as my Lord and Savior. I believe that your son Jesus Christ was born of the Virgin Mary, was crucified and died on the cross at Calvary for us. I believe that after the 3 days he raised from the dead, ascended into Heaven, and is alive today. I ask you Jesus Christ to be my Lord and Savior of my life. I receive you now as my Lord and Savior with all of my heart. I believe that Jesus Christ is my King and my God and the Lord of my life. I believe that Jesus Christ is alive in me, and I declare that Jesus Christ is the Lord of my Life. Amen!

WHAT DID YOUR YES COST YOU? We would love to hear your stories. Email us at whatmyyescostme@yahoo.com

About the Author

Corliss Webb Collins is the Author of "What my Yes Cost Me". Her desire is to inspire individuals to overcome their past mistakes and help pull them out of bondage. Corliss is an Overcomer and caring, loveable person. She is an Inspiring and Motivational Speaker.

Before, Corliss became an inspiring Author. She spent a small amount of time in the Entrepreneurship area along with achieving the goal of become a Nurse in spite of circumstances she was faced with. But, most of all she loves spending time with her loving husband Antago and family along with traveling the world and exploring new fun adventures together, and meeting new people. Corliss and Antago resides in Houston, TX.

Made in the USA
Middletown, DE
09 October 2021